INVERTEBRATES

INVERTEBRATES
by Nathan Aaseng

A Venture Book
FRANKLIN WATTS
New York · Chicago · London · Toronto · Sydney

JERICHO PUBLIC LIBRARY

Photographs copyright ©: Animals Animals: pp. 14 (Peter Parks/OSF), 22 (Fred Whitehead), 24 top(Carl Roessler), 24 bottom (Mickey Gibson), 34 (R. F. Head), 36 top (Tim Rock), 36 bottom (W. Gregory Brown), 46 (J. H. Robinson), 50 (E. R. Degginger), 57 (Robert Maier), 59 (Kathie Atkinson/OSF), 70 (Robert Redden), 77, 98 (all Zig Leszczynski), 80 (Stan Schoeder), 86 (Carson Baldwin, Jr.) 90 (John A. Novak), 92 (Patti Murray); Visuals Unlimited: pp. 17 (K. G. Murti), 31 (John Forsythe), 38, 54, 68 (all John D. Cunningham), 44 (T. E. Adams).

Library of Congress Cataloging-in-Publication Data

Aaseng, Nathan.
Invertebrates/Nathan Aaseng.
Includes bibliographical references and index.
Summary: Discusses animals with no backbones, including protozoans, sponges, worms, mollusks, arachnids, and arthropods.
ISBN 0-531-12550-5
1. Invertebrates—Juvenile literature. [1.Invertebrates.] I. Title.
QL362.4.A27   1993
592—dc20   93-4093 CIP AC

Copyright © 1993 by Nathan Aaseng
All rights reserved
Printed in the United States of America
5 4 3 2 1

CONTENTS

To Doc Roslien and
the Biology Department
at Luther College

INTRODUCTION

If we were making a motion picture and were assigning parts to the animals of the earth, most of us would probably cast humans in the starring roles. Other mammals, birds, and maybe reptiles, fish, and amphibians would get supporting roles. Somehow we usually think of these as the "most important" animals.

The invertebrates would probably be lumped together as what Hollywood calls extras. They would be the bit players who make up the crowd in the background, have no speaking roles, and are lucky if they are even listed in the credits.

The fact is, we often view invertebrates as bit players in the animal world. For the most part, these are small animals we seldom see or think about. Those we encounter most often, such as flies and mosquitoes, are considered nuisances. Few invertebrates contribute anything that we hold to be valuable.

Scientists have not helped the invertebrates' poor

reputation. They speak of them as the "lower" animals. They have given them a name, invertebrates, that describes them only by saying what they are missing. Invertebrates means "animals without backbones"; this sets them apart from the vertebrates, the "higher" animals who have backbones.

Such talk can give the impression that invertebrates are outdated models who have been left in the dust by far superior animals. It seems that these animals have no more hope of competing with us higher animals than primitive spears against a modern air force.

The numbers, however, tell a different story. In the race for survival, invertebrates completely dominate the vertebrates. Roughly one and a half million different species of animals have been isolated on earth. More than 95 percent of those are invertebrates. One group of invertebrates alone, the insects, make up two-thirds of all living species.

Invertebrates have penetrated virtually every type of environment on earth, from oceans and fresh water to deserts, polar ice caps, soil, and even the insides of other creatures. They range in size from tiny, one-celled creatures too small to be seen without a microscope to the 60-foot (18.29 m) giant squid. Despite our best efforts to destroy them, many invertebrate pests thrive as well as ever. Contrast this with the many species of vertebrates who, despite the efforts of some humans to save them, are fighting for their survival, are in danger of extinction. In view of the invertebrates' survival success, it would be more to the point to describe invertebrates as simpler or less complex forms of life rather than lower forms of life.

Actually, there is no dividing line in nature that separates animals into vertebrate and invertebrate groups. Such divisions are human inventions designed to organize the world into some kind of order so that we can begin to make sense of it. In order to understand how the earth's creatures all fit together, we sort them into groups that are similar.

Scientists sort animals by looking at such things as body shape, complexity, and the ways in which an animal has adapted to meet the needs of survival: how they get food and oxygen, reproduce, move, gain information from the environment, and defend themselves.

Life-forms on earth are so diverse that experts have trouble sorting out and classifying even the broadest groupings. As we will see with the protozoans, even the basic difference between a plant and an animal is not always clear-cut. In many ways, sorting and classifying animals is like working on a 3-million-piece jigsaw puzzle with about half the pieces missing. The task is so enormously difficult that experts are bound to disagree every step of the way.

The animal kingdom is divided into major groups called *phyla* (the singular form is *phylum*). Of all the phyla identified, only one—the chordates—includes vertebrates. All the rest, and experts claim anywhere from twenty to thirty-eight different phyla, are invertebrates.

Within different phyla, animals are further divided into classes, which are divided into orders, which are divided into families, which are divided into genera, which are divided into species. A species can be defined as an interbreeding group distinct from all others and unable to breed with other similar groups. Life-forms on earth are so diverse that disagreements arise in all categories and prompt some experts to further divide into suborders, subspecies, and so on.

What is the point of getting mixed up in this overwhelming jigsaw puzzle of nature, and especially with invertebrates? The first reason is simply to satisfy our curiosity about these creatures, many of them invisible and unknown to us, with whom we share the planet.

Second, as frustrating as it may be to sort out the

species, an understanding of the relationships among animals will give us a better understanding of our world. It will tell us why the world is the way it is and why animals are the way they are.

Finally, studying the relationships among animals will help us to understand ourselves—why we are the way we are and where we fit in this marvelously complex world. Since invertebrates make up the vast majority of animal life, we can barely skim the surface of these issues without including them in our study.

1
PROTOZOANS: ONE-CELLED ORGANISMS

All living things are made up of *cells*, tiny, individually distinct masses of living matter. A protozoan, which consists of a single cell operating as an independent unit, is the simplest form of invertebrate life. Yet protozoans are in some ways more complex than animals composed of collections of cells.

Protozoans lie so far at the edge of the animal kingdom that most biologists are not even convinced they *are* animals. Some protozoans, *Euglena* for example, contain chlorophyll and are able to *photosynthesize*, to use light energy to manufacture food. This is a characteristic of green plants. Many other protozoans are free-moving, and can capture and digest food from outside sources. These are characteristics of animals. The fact that protozoans can act like both plants and animals has prompted most biologists to separate these single-celled organisms from both groups and put them into their own kingdom, Protista.

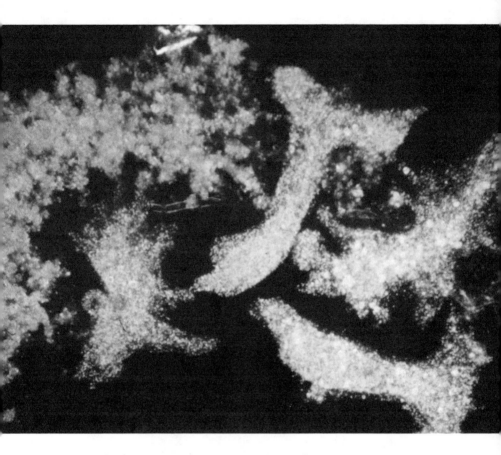

This microscopic photograph, magnified many times, shows an amoeba feeding on green plant material.

Because they are so small, protozoans are seldom noticed by humans. Yet they live all around us and, in some cases, inside us. More than 60,000 species have been described. About two dozen of these make their home in the human body. Perhaps 10,000 more species live as parasites on other animals. The rest are free-living creatures who inhabit streams, ponds, and, in lesser

14

numbers, large lakes and oceans. They are also commonly found in such household locations as plant pots and aquariums.

Protozoans, as a group, have proven to be adaptable. They can adapt to habitats as diverse as polar ice caps and sewers. The main restriction on their range is that they need to be surrounded by moisture. But they do not need much moisture—protozoans can even live in the delicate film of water that surrounds soil particles.

Since protozoans consist of a single cell, somehow that cell must find a way to perform all the functions needed to survive. One of the most basic functions of any living thing is obtaining food. Protozoans accomplish this in various ways. Some of them are filter-feeders, which means that they strain suspended particles from water. They use tiny hairs called *cilia* to beat a current of water that draws in bacteria and some larger material. Most protozoans do not have digestive systems. They simply absorb food through thin body membranes.

This kind of absorption is possible only with a special kind of structure that will allow some material to pass through yet provide a barrier to other material. The protozoan cell membrane freely allows water and tiny food particles to pass through but keeps larger molecules from passing out or in. If it did not do this, protozoans would be unable to prevent their own proteins from leaking away.

Some protozoans, such as the amoeba, are tiny predators. Amoebas look like irregular blobs of jelly contained in a thin membrane. They can produce a two-way flow of cellular protoplasm that pushes out portions of their cell walls in extensions called *pseudopods* (false feet). When they discover a food source, amoebas send out pseudopods to surround it. The food becomes enclosed in a food cup. This food cup is drawn into the body where it becomes a food vacuole and digests the captured food.

15

Many protozoans have found it easier to live off the food that some other creature has collected than to gather their own. They attach themselves to a ready food source within that creature and live as parasites.

Another basic function of animals is the ability to move within their environment in order to get food. Protozoans do not move quickly, but they do have a variety of methods of slow movement. Amoebas travel by extending their pseudopods and then pulling the rest of the cell up to the pseudopods. A group of protozoans known as flagellates rely on the action of a threadlike whip, or flagellum, to propell them through water. Another group, the ciliates, advance by means of cilia that pull the organism through the water like tiny oars.

Even the simplest of animals requires some basic way of coordinating its food-gathering and moving activities. Protozoans, too, need some way of gathering and interpreting information about the environment in order to detect the presence of food. More complex multi-celled creatures have complex nervous systems to handle these functions. Protozoans rely on highly specialized *organelles* within the cell. These tiny cellular structures can detect chemicals in the environment around them and stimulate a reaction to those chemicals in the animals.

Animals convert food into usable energy by a chemical process that requires oxygen. Protozoans can absorb oxygen through their membrane walls, and have organelles called *mitochondria* that convert oxygen and food molecules into biochemical energy.

Because organisms are constantly bringing material into their bodies, they also must remove wastes—unused or unusable material—that builds up. Freshwater protozoans tend to absorb water by *osmosis*. Osmosis is a process by which water flows through a membrane so as to balance the concentration of dissolved material on either side of the membrane. Osmosis, for example,

The organelles known as mitochondria
are able to convert oxygen and food
into energy for the protozoan to use.

would cause a cell that contains a higher concentration of salt than the surrounding water to absorb water. If this went on unchecked, it could damage or destroy the cell membranes. To counter this, protozoans have contractile vacuoles that pump out excess water.

Protozoans have few methods of avoiding or discouraging capture by larger predators. A few protozoans in both fresh water and the ocean release into the water a toxic substance that kills fish. Some parasites have developed ways to survive in the digestive tracts of other animals without being digested. But other than that, their survival as a group depends on their ability to reproduce rapidly.

Most protozoans are neither one sex nor the other. They reproduce by simple cell division (called *fission*) that is governed by the nucleus. Reproduction occurs when the cell develops a second nucleus and then splits in two, with both new cells performing as individual protozoans. Some amoebas are surrounded by shells that cannot be split off so easily. In some cases, the original cell gets the shell while the new amoeba forms a new shell. In others, the old shell is discarded completely and both of the protozoans emerging from the split develop new shells.

Under favorable conditions, when food and water are available, a protozoan can grow and divide again in less than an hour. But for an organism to be successful over a long period of time, it cannot depend on favorable conditions. Some one-celled animals have developed a backup plan for when water is not available. They secrete a hard covering over the newly formed individuals. In this encysted stage, protozoans can lie dormant in the absence of water, and so survive until water returns to their environment.

Some protozoans are parasitic; that is, they feed off other living things. Parasitic protozoans have developed specialized life cycles to ensure their survival. This often requires that they spend different parts of their lives inside different animals.

Humans seldom directly encounter protozoans in the everyday course of life. Several of the parasitic species, however, cause a great deal of misery. The most destructive are four species of the genus *Plasmodium*; these are responsible for the disease malaria. These organisms undergo what might appear to be a chancy life cycle. They can grow into adulthood only by locating exactly the right host at two different stages in their lives. First, they have to find their way to a mosquito of a particular variety. Then they have to be transferred to humans. The odds of both these events happening might seem to be great, but enough *Plasmodium* have completed the cycle to make malaria a major cause of death and illness worldwide.

Once in the human body, *Plasmodium* invade individual blood cells. They feed on the contents of those cells, grow, and reproduce by cell fission. At some point, so many *Plasmodium* are produced that the blood cell ruptures, sending the protozoans out into the bloodstream. There each finds another red blood cell to infect. Reproduction is apparently synchronized in the animals so that many blood cells rupture at the same time. The body's immune system tries to combat this by raising the body temperature. This causes the fever that is common with malaria. *Plasmodium* destroy so many blood cells that the victim is weakened and often dies.

Once certain kinds of mosquitoes were identified as carriers of the *Plasmodium* species, the disease could be attacked by destroying their breeding grounds. Malaria has been eliminated in the United States by this method. However, *Plasmodium*-induced malaria continues to be a major concern in many parts of Africa and Asia. In 1991, nearly 2 million people died of malaria, making it one of the most serious health problems in the world.

African sleeping sickness is also caused by protozoans. This disease is caused by a group of one-celled animals known as *trypanosomes*, which are transmitted by the tsetse fly. Trypanosomes thrive on human blood and can cause brain damage or death.

Another type of protozoan makes it possible for termites to damage human dwellings. Termites, by themselves, are unable to digest the tough cellulose fibers that make up much of the structural material in wood. Their digestive systems, however, commonly contain a flagellate protozoan that can digest the wood and help the termite to gain nutrients from it.

But protozoans also perform services that are valuable to humans. They produce a great deal of organic matter that is especially important in sustaining a variety of life in aquatic environments. They are useful in helping to break down or decompose material. Waste treatment plants make use of this ability. Raw sewage is treated with protozoans that break down the sewage into material that can be more easily dispersed into the environment without polluting rivers and lakes.

Protozoans have been able to survive in great numbers because they can reproduce rapidly and because they require few resources to supply their tiny bodies. But their single-cell body plan has certain limitations. Single-celled animals cannot grow much beyond microscopic size. A single cell can accomplish only so much in trying to provide all the functions an organism requires. When one cell has to provide all the functions needed by an organism, it cannot perform all the tasks as efficiently and effectively as specialized cells, each performing a single function. Protozoans are limited to very basic means of movement and interacting with their environment.

Protozoans often seek out other organisms to share some of their work load. This leads to the type of mutually helpful arrangement that exists between termites and the protozoans in their digestive systems. In a few cases, such as with the *Chrysomonadina*, protozoans form colonies, large collections of animals that band together to obtain food and other necessities more efficiently.

2
PORIFERA: SPONGES

The more that colonies of single-celled animals function as a single unit rather than just a collection of individuals, the more they begin to resemble multi-celled animals. The phylum known as Porifera bridges the gap between single-cell and multi-cell animals.

This group, commonly known as the sponges, includes an estimated 5,000 to 10,000 species. Sponges live in water, most of them in the ocean. Because many of them cannot survive for even a short period of time out of water, they are usually not found along shores where a low tide leaves them exposed to the air. Sponges have been found at depths of up to 28,000 feet (8,600 m), but most of them thrive best in warm, shallow seas. Only two families of porifera live in fresh water.

For thousands of years, sponges were prized for their ability to soak up and hold water. This made them valuable cleaning tools. In more recent years, however, natural sponges have been replaced by artificial substitutes that are cheaper to produce.

21

The phylum Porifera is another example of the problems zoologists have in trying to separate and classify animals. Sponges were considered to be plants until the eighteenth century, when a few researchers began to cast doubt on that belief. Only in the nineteenth century did scientists begin to agree that sponges were more properly grouped among the animals.

Sponges are difficult animals to study. They cannot be completely understood by looking at their individual cells under a microscope. They also cannot be understood very well by dissecting them, or opening them up to see what is inside. Sponges act very much like colonies of single-celled animals that have developed an organized method of working together. There is no evidence that sponges are even remotely related to any other group of animals. Some experts believe that sponges are so different from both protozoans and more complex animals that they should be put in a separate animal sub-kingdom, Parazoa.

It is not surprising that sponges were considered plants for so many years. Like plants, they live attached to the rocks or sediment at the bottom of a body of water. And sponges *look* more like plants than animals. They have no eyes, mouth, or visible appendages, such as the arms or legs we normally associate with animals. Many of them are brightly colored; some of them are branched or even fan-shaped. Some varieties are flat and cover the surface of rocks like moss or lichen. They are generally asymmetrical, which means that they have an irregular shape. Like plants, a sponge's appearance can be af-

This display of natural sponges for sale in a Florida fishing village illustrates the variety of forms within the phylum Porifera.

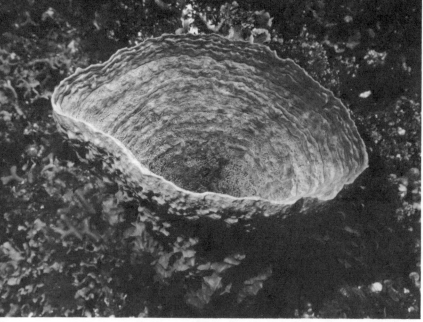

fected by the environment in which it lives. The strength of the water currents and the type of ground to which it is anchored greatly influence its body form.

Sponges appear to be a special adaptation of cells for the purpose of filter-feeding. In the oceans, a great deal of food is available in the form of *plankton*. Plankton refers to a broad group of tiny, often microscopic, plants and animals that float in the ocean. But while plankton is plentiful, it is diluted by the enormous amount of ocean water. On the average, the oceans contain less than 1 milligram of plankton per liter. An animal that sought out and captured plankton one at a time would use up more energy getting the food than it would receive, and would quickly starve. A plankton eater can make the process far more energy-efficient by pumping in large amounts of water and straining out the plankton. Single-celled protozoans can do this by producing a very small water flow with their cilia. But a far more efficient pumping and filtering system can be created by a large collection of cells.

Sponges have developed in a number of ways that help make them successful filter-feeders. Basically, sponges consist of a chamber surrounded by walls made up of two layers of cells. A jellylike substance can usually be found between the two walls. The phylum name, Porifera, means "pore bearers" and refers to the many small openings that connect the outside of the wall to the inside.

The cells on the inner surface of the sponge wall

Two varieties of sponges that look more like exotic plants than animals: the yellow tube sponge (above) and the barrel sponge (below).

25

are called *choanocytes*. They are equipped with flagella similar to those found on some protozoans. In fact, these cells often closely resemble protozoans. Their flagella can create a current that draws water into the sponge through the pores. Most sponges also depend on natural currents to provide a water flow. The current flows through the pores into canals and into the chamber, an open space in the middle of the sponge's body. The larger the sponge, the more complex the series of canals and chambers.

As the water passes through the sponge, the choanocytes that line the chamber trap food in a filtering unit known as a *collar*, a structure that resembles a group of tentacles. Since sponges do not have mouths for taking in food, the choanocyte captures the trapped food. The captured food is then enclosed in a food vacuole, similar to those of protozoans, and is digested. Choanocytes are capable of passing along digested food to other sponge cells. But because they have no organized system of digestion, sponges cannot take in food larger than can be engulfed by a single cell.

Along with an efficient means of collecting plankton, sponges have developed a simple way to get rid of the excess water that flows in. After the water reaches the chamber, it is simply pumped out of the sponge through a single opening called the *osculum*.

A single cell requires no supporting structure other than a thin cell membrane to separate its insides from the outside. But a sponge's system of pores, canals, and chambers would collapse in a heap without something solid to help it maintain its rigid form. Sponges have two types of skeletons that support them. Many contain a flexible type of fiber known as *spongin*. This is a soft material similar to foam rubber that gives the sponges their characteristic soft, elastic quality. Many sponges also form hard, brittle material known as *spicules* that give strength to their supporting structures. Generally made from calcium carbonate, a salt commonly found in nature, these spicules can be found in a variety of shapes ranging from needles to stars.

The spicules and spongin linger on in the sponge long after death. They give the sponge its shape and are especially useful in helping biologists identify different species of sponges.

Because their food floats to them in water currents, porifera have no need for mobility. Instead, they require a firm base from which to operate. Rather than developing a means of locomotion, they have developed ways to anchor themselves to one spot. Some sponges are even capable of boring into rocks to give themselves a firm foundation.

Other than their system for taking in food and disposing of excess water, sponges are not much more complex than protozoans. They have no system of nerves to help them gain information from or react to their environment. The individual cells are capable of only very basic responses. For example, many sponges close up when touched. But their response is slow, and there is little evidence that they interact with their environment in any other way.

Since their cells always have a surface exposed to water, sponges have no need for a respiratory system. Any oxygen required for turning food to energy can be pulled in from the surrounding water.

Sponges are preyed upon by a number of sea creatures, including fish, starfish, turtles, and slugs. They have developed some defenses to protect themselves against these attacks. The sharp spicules discourage many potential predators. Many sponges also contain chemicals that are poisonous to fish. A few varieties can sting an unwary human handler.

Reproduction for a multi-celled animal is not quite as simple as for a single cell that can split in two to form a new animal. Many types of sponges take asexual

27

reproduction to a more complex step. *Budding* occurs when a section or outgrowth of the sponge grows until it is the size of the parent sponge. Sometimes these buds break off and grow on their own, and sometimes they remain attached as part of a sponge colony. This type of new cell formation allows sponges to regenerate parts that become broken or damaged.

Some sponges, especially those with shorter life spans, ensure their survival with a delayed form of reproduction. These sponges produce small internal buds called *gemmules*. While the parent sponge dies during the winter, the gemmules survive and grow into new sponges in the spring, when conditions are more favorable.

Because porifera are no longer commercially important, we seldom encounter them. Yet they continue to thrive in the ocean. In many cases, they are almost identical to colonies of single-celled protozoans. But their two-layered body wall has demonstrated one important advantage of multi-celled animals over single-cell creatures. The outside layer of cells stands between the inside layer and the outside environment. This provides a controlled internal environment that shields the inside cells from variable outside conditions. The next group of animals shows how cells in this type of protected environment can begin to organize on a slightly more complex level than the sponges.

3
CNIDARIANS

The next group of animals is more familiar to humans, especially to ocean swimmers. While sponges generally live out of harm's way on the ocean bottom, cnidarians (the c is silent) float around in the water and wash up on the sand. Humans wading in oceans or walking along beaches occasionally encounter these creatures, with painful results.

Although only a few of the cnidarians are dangerous, they cause hundreds of human deaths each year, more than are caused by sharks. One box-shaped cnidarian, a jellyfish called the sea wasp, contains one of the most deadly poisons known. Even when diluted 10,000 times it can kill laboratory animals in seconds.

As we have seen, the animal kingdom does not divide itself into neat, distinct groups. The progression from simple to complex animals is also not an orderly sequence. Cnidarians are not related to porifera, but they are usually listed next in the sequence of animals because they have taken the simple multi-celled form and added features not found in sponges.

Cnidarians include an estimated 10,000 species as diverse as coral, sea anemones, and jellyfish. They share a number of similarities with the porifera. They occupy the same habitat, primarily the ocean, with a few species thriving in fresh water. Their body construction is similar—two layers of cells that contain a filling of a gelatinous substance called *mesoglea*. Like the sponges, the cnidarians' cells all have at least one surface in contact with water. This means that they can obtain the oxygen needed for energy release and can remove waste products obtained from converting food to energy (such as carbon dioxide) by diffusing these molecules through their cell walls.

The cnidarians were formerly known as the *coelenterates*, from the Latin for "hollow gut." This refers to an open space in the middle of the body that is more complex than the chambers of the sponges. Unlike the porifera chamber, which mainly serves to collect the food-bearing water pumped in through the pores, the protected inner environment of the cnidarians contains cells specially organized to play a more active role in digestion.

Cnidarians tend to funnel food into the digestive cavity through a single opening rather than through many pores as do the sponges. This opening, the mouth, is usually surrounded by tentacles that capture prey and direct them to the mouth. Cnidarian tentacles can be compared to fishing lines. They extend out from the cnidarian into the water and hang limply, waiting for a fish

Humans have died within minutes from the sting of the sea wasp's tentacles.

30

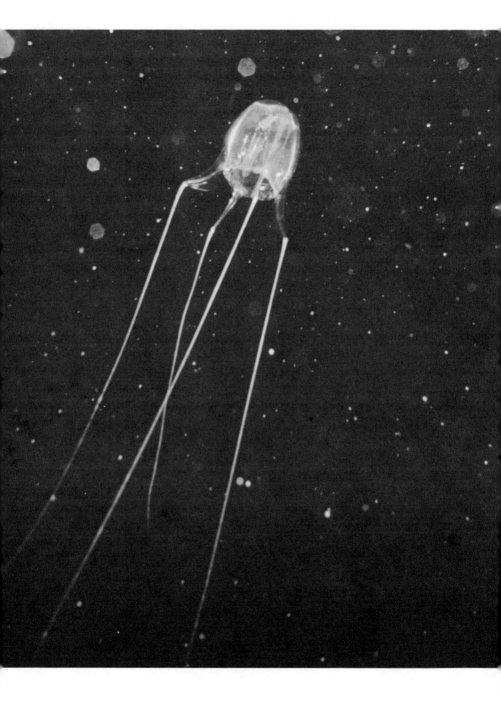

or smaller animal to bump into them. On contact, the tentacles grasp the prey and reel it in to the mouth.

The development of the mouth leads to a more definite, balanced shape in cnidarians. Body shapes do not need to be uniform in sponges because food comes into the animal from many directions. Cnidarians, however, tend to be arranged around that one important food-gathing opening. This leads to a body form known as *radial symmetry*, which can be likened to spokes radiating out from the hub of a wheel. No matter where the animal is cut in half along a single plane, the two sides will be alike.

Cnidarians contain more specialized cells than are found in Porifera. The advantage of this is that each cell does not have to perform all the survival functions of the animal. Cells with similar functions in cnidarians are arranged into tissues that can perform one special function more efficiently.

Anemones, coral, and jellyfish have a basic nervous system that features specialized nerve cells called *cnido-blasts*. This unique feature is what gives the phylum its name. Cnidoblasts contain capsules called *nematocysts*, or stinging cells. A nematocyst is like a jack-in-the-box with a hollow thread folded or coiled inside. Cnidoblasts are equipped with triggers that stimulate the nematocysts when they detect the presence of another animal. The coiled threads then spring out through a trapdoor on one end of the nematocyst, unfolding at blinding speed.

These threads are used both for food gathering and for protection against enemies. Some cnidoblasts are capable of stunning or killing their prey; others wrap up the victim and bring it to the mouth. Cnidoblasts are not linked by a central nervous system that coordinates all of the animal's stinging activity. Each stinging cell is stimulated and discharged independently. For that reason, jellyfish can discharge cnidoblasts and cause painful injuries even when dead.

Cnidarians can reproduce asexually by budding, as do the sponges. But most are also capable of sexual reproduction. Sexual reproduction provides the advantage of variety and adaptability. Organisms that simply split off from a parent have characteristics identical to those of the parent. Sexual reproduction, on the other hand, can combine features of two different animals to create new combinations. Some of these new combinations prove to be more useful for survival than the single-parent characteristics.

Another unique feature of cnidarian reproduction is that many of these animals have two phases to their life cycle. One form, considered the adult form in jellyfish, is the *medusa*. A medusa floats or swims in the water in the shape of a bell or umbrella. The tentacles hang downward from the edge of the umbrella and bring food up to its mouth, which is in the center of the lower surface.

The other form is the polyp, in which the body is almost completely reversed. Polyps consist of a plantlike stalk or stem that is usually attached to a surface, such as a rock. The mouth faces upward and the tentacles rise around it like branches on a tree. Coral, sea anemone, and immature jellyfish take this form.

The most common cnidarian classes are Anthozoa, Scyphozoa, and Hydrozoa. Anthozoans include corals and sea anemones. These are the cnidarians that share the most characteristics with the sponges. They often more closely resemble plants than flowers; in fact, the word *anthozoa* means "flower animals." They are often brightly colored and lack any outwardly recognizable characteristics of animals.

Anthozoans exist only in the polyp form. Like sponges, they do not float freely but must either attach themselves to rocks and other objects or burrow into the sea bottom. They are primarily filter-feeders who catch what comes to them. They aid this process by creating a

The fleshy tentacles of this sea anemone resemble
the petals of a flower. This animal anchors itself
to a surface by secreting a gluelike substance.

water flow to help transport food into their bodies. Food is captured by tentacles lined with heavy secretions of mucus; these act like flypaper to trap tiny particles of suspended food.

Sea anemones are hollow cylinders topped by a mouth surrounded by many fleshy tentacles; these tentacles give it its flower appearance.

Corals are small polyps that usually live together in large colonies. Each polyp builds a shelter made of the same stony material (calcium carbonate) used by sponges to form spicules. When corals die, the next generation of corals builds upon the old structures. The beautiful shapes and stunning colors of these coral colonies make them a prime attraction for divers. Over thousands of years, some colonies have formed in such masses that they have created great reefs and thousands of small islands in the Pacific Ocean.

Many corals have developed a survival advantage by cooperating with other organisms. Some coral cells contain microscopic green algae. These plants help the coral by using photosynthesis to convert coral waste products into nutrients the coral can use.

Scyphozoa means "cap animals," and is named after the floating parachute that gives jellyfish their distinctive shape. Jellyfish are more active hunters than anthozoans. Rather than laying in wait for their food, they float in the ocean currents and can even swim on their own through a coordinated effort of their limited nervous and muscle systems. Jellyfish catch their prey, invertebrates and small fish, by paralyzing them with their cnidoblasts. These stingers are powerful enough to cause painful welts on humans who accidentally bump into them. The weight of their captured food can make it difficult for them to float, so they break down their food quickly in a digestive chamber.

Some cnidarians show the beginnings of organized nerve systems that help them interact with their environ-

The many beautiful and varied shapes of corals are illustrated by this leather coral (left) and mushroom coral (below). Corals have been so numerous in the sea that their remains created the 1,200-mile-long Great Barrier Reef near Australia.

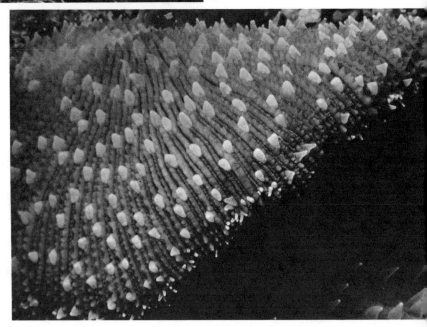

ment. Some jellyfish can detect differences in sunlight. They can then adjust their floating depth to put them where the most plants are likely to be found. Some show very basic signs of coordinated physical activity, such as a system of balance receptors to keep them floating upright and an ability to swim slowly through rhythmic contractions.

The familiar form of the jellyfish is the *medusa*. The jellyfish medusa has special areas inside the body wall in which eggs and sperm are produced. The eggs and sperm are released into the sea, where fertilization takes place. The tiny developing embryo swims for a short time by using cilia. Then it drops to the bottom, finds a place to attach itself, and grows into a polyp. The polyp form is able to reproduce by asexual budding. By alternating generations of sexual and asexual reproduction, jellyfish gain the advantages of both. A huge number of new animals can be produced from one parent, yet some variety is also introduced.

The alternating polyp-medusa forms also help jellyfish to survive a variety of conditions. Living on the ocean bottom, the polyp is better able to survive the winter storms that destroy the medusa form. Medusas rarely live as long as a year, while polyps can survive for several years.

Hydrozoa include one of the most fascinating of the cnidarians, the Portuguese man-of-war. This animal floats on the surface of the ocean, held up by a colorful, gas-inflated bag made of thin skin. The bag can be as large as 15.5 inches (40 cm) in diameter and is rimmed with long, stinging tentacles that dangle down several feet. The stingers kill and capture prey, and are especially hazardous to swimmers and beachcombers along the Caribbean. The Portuguese man-of-war has a delicate system of balance that enables it to tip the bag to one side and then the other every few minutes to keep the bag from drying out.

The Portuguese man-of-war
was so named because
its floating bag reminded
sailors of a type of ship
sailed by the Portuguese. Its
poison is nearly as powerful
as that of a cobra.

So far in our study we have not encountered an animal capable of living on land. The fact that simpler animals are overwhelmingly marine creatures leads biologists to speculate that all animal life originated in the sea.

As compared to the sponges and protozoans, the cnidarians have moved a short way along a path that could lead to survival on land. The cnidarians' body cavity, in which specific functions are carried out by a group of similar cells, is a small step in the direction of internal body systems.

4
PLATYHELMINTHES: FLATWORMS

An animal with only an inside and an outside layer of cells, such as a sponge or cnidarian, has a limited chance of creating a controlled internal environment with specialized parts. The phylum Platyhelminthes provides more raw material for internal body parts by adding a third layer of cells between the external and internal layers.

Platyhelminthes means "flatworm." There are an estimated 15,000 species of flatworms in the world. One group, the turbellarians, consists of small, free-living hunters. They are harmless and are scarcely noticed by humans in the normal course of life. Two other groups, however, the cestodes and the trematodes, are parasitic and include humans among their victims. Many people find these flatworms so disgusting in both their appearance and their life cycles that they get squeamish just thinking about them.

Flatworms' bodies are constructed for the task of

survival, not for show. These animals are not filter-feeders who stay in one spot and wait for food to arrive. They move in search of food. This basic change in food-gathering strategy gives the animal the advantage of being less dependent on one local environment to meet its needs. It requires a body that is radically different from the sponges and cnidarians. The most obvious of these changes is body shape. Animals that are anchored to one spot have no need of a front or back end. They can be asymmetrical, like sponges, or radially symmetrical, like sea anemones. When an animal moves in a particular direction, however, one end leads the other.

The development of a front and a rear end have led to two trends in the more complex animals: cephalization and bilateral symmetry. Cephalization means the development of a head, a forward place in which nerves and senses are concentrated. Again, creatures that stay in one spot have no particular need for a head. They do not encounter their environment more often at any one place than another, so it makes more sense to have their means of gaining information from the environment spread out.

An animal that moves forward into new environments, however, always has one end that encounters this new environment first. This head end is the one that first comes in contact with possible prey and predators. It makes sense for that animal to concentrate its means of sampling the environment on that front end so that it can quickly identify both danger and opportunity.

Flatworms have moved in this direction. Although free-living flatworms have chemical-sensing cells scattered throughout their bodies, a greater percentage of these cells are located in the head. The planarian's nervous system and sensory mechanisms are also concentrated in the head. In addition, a parasitic flatworm may have a special structure on its front end to help gather food.

41

Bilateral symmetry means that there is only one line along which the animal can be cut to produce two equal, mirror-image pieces. Any other cut will produce dissimilar pieces. Animals that have a definite front and back end have bilateral symmetry. Such animals have a right and a left side. Bilateral animals do not always show perfect symmetry. Humans, for example, have the heart located on the left side with no mirror organ on the right. But we are considered bilaterally symmetrical because we have a front and rear, right and left side. Bilaterally symmetrical beings are seldom spherical like sponges or jellyfish. Rather, they tend to be streamlined, with the body flattened out and lengthened. This streamlined form provides less resistance to forward movement so that the animal can move more quickly. A long, thin, flexible body is especially useful for parasitic flatworms. It helps them to burrow into animal tissues to exploit the food available there.

Independent movement also requires a way to provide locomotion that is more efficient than the flagella or cilia found in simpler animals. Free-living flatworms still use cilia to help provide motion—in fact, they may be covered with millions of them. But they have also developed a contracting tissue in the form of muscles. This muscle tissue comes from that third layer of cells. Muscles also add more bulk and structural support than the mesoglea of the cnidarians could provide.

Along with muscles, flatworms have developed a more complex nervous system to coordinate the movements of these muscles. Flatworms are capable of several forms of locomotion, including swimming, gliding, creeping, and wriggling.

Flatworms do not have a body cavity to provide a sheltered internal environment for their cells. But they do go beyond cnidarians in cell specialization. Whereas similar cells in cnidarians could develop into tissues, flatworms have tissues that are organized into more complex and efficient structures called *organs*.

42

Flatworms remain similar to the simpler animals in that they have no oxygen-collecting respiratory system or circulation system to distribute oxygen all over the body. The flatness of their bodies leaves them with a high ratio of surface area to volume; in other words, most of their body cells are at or near the surface rather than buried beneath layers of cells. This makes it possible for direct oxygen and carbon dioxide exchange between the cells and their environment.

Most reproduction among flatworms is sexual, but some also reproduce without fertilization. Most flatworms that reproduce sexually have both male and female sex organs in the same individual. Some of the parasites have developed complicated life cycles that require them to penetrate a different host organism at two or three stages of their lives.

The best known of the free-living flatworms is the planaria, commonly used in science experiments. A planarian's organs include a pair of simple "eyes" located near the front end. These eye spots help in gaining information from the environment, such as the presence of light and food. Planarians also have a bundle of nerves concentrated in a simple brain in the head that can process this information and direct the response of the muscles. The ability of the planarian's brain to learn from the information provided and to remember previous experiences helps it to survive in a hostile world.

Despite the fact that planarians have developed a front or head end, their mouths are located near the middle of their bodies rather than the front end. A planarian detects food with the sensory equipment in its head, then inserts the pharynx, or food tube, into its prey. The pharynx digests the food into smaller pieces that can be finished off in the digestive cavity. The waste products of digestion are excreted back through the mouth opening. Planarians also have an excretory system to remove liquid waste products. This consists of a network of *flame cells* that run down the length of the body; these filter

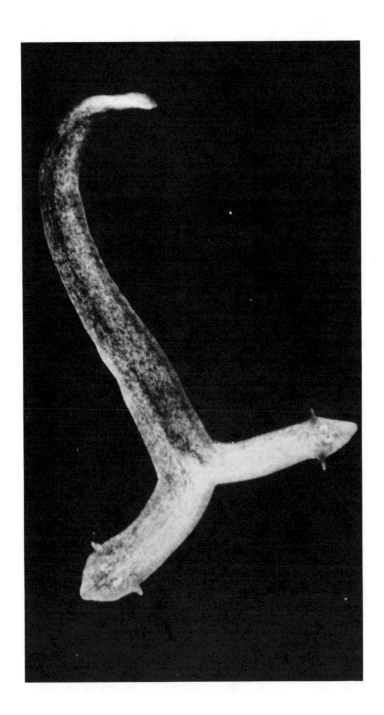

body fluids and dispose of them through pores leading out of the body.

Planarians are known for their astounding ability to regenerate body parts. If sliced down the middle of the head, right between the eyes, each side will grow into a complete new head. The two-headed planarian will then usually split into two separate creatures.

Trematodes are a group of parasitic flatworms commonly known as flukes. Flukes get their nutrients from digesting the internal tissue of larger animals. Adult flukes have suckers that enable them to attach themselves to host tissue. Flukes usually must go through three hosts, one of which is generally a freshwater snail, in order to complete their life cycles. The chances of an immature fluke finding these animals at the right stage of life are not good. Because of this, a mature fluke will produce enormous quantities of fertilized eggs, as many as 300 a day, to ensure that a few survive.

One kind of fluke, the schistosome, is responsible for the disease schistosomiasis, one of the most widespread diseases that plague humans. Schistosomes live inside the human body and feed on blood. They rarely cause death but leave their host extremely tired and weak. This disease affects an estimated 200 million people, almost all exclusively in the tropics.

Cestodes are a group of parasitic flatworms known as tapeworms that live in the digestive tracts of their hosts. They feature a specialized head called a *scolex*.

Planarians are known for their ability to regenerate, or regrow, body parts. This flatworm's head has split in two. Eventually, its entire body will split to form two separate creatures.

45

This parasitic tapeworm once lived in the digestive system of a cat, absorbing the nutrients that the animal digested.

Like other flatworm heads, the scolex contains a concentration of nerves, but it also has suckers or hooks that it uses to latch on to the host.

Tapeworms have no digestive tract because they have shortcut the process of eating. They let the host do the eating and digesting for them. They live in the host's digestive tract and simply absorb the nutrients from the digested food. Tapeworms avoid being digested themselves, apparently by producing a substance that prevents the host's protein-digesting enzymes from acting on them.

Tapeworms produce buds from the area behind the head, with each new segment added on to the body like another link in a chain. Tapeworms sometimes act as a single individual, but at other times they seem to be more like colonies of these segments. Each segment contains male and female organs and can absorb its own nutrients directly. Tapeworms can keep adding segments until they are as long as 40 feet. (12 m).

Tapeworms are found most often in sheep and cattle. Only a few species of tapeworms attack humans, who become infected by eating raw or undercooked fish containing the flatworms.

5
NEMATODES: ROUNDWORMS

Nematodes, the roundworms, are among the most numerous and successful groups of animals on earth. Millions of nematodes can be found in a square yard of sea mud; an acre of rich farmland may contain billions. One patient scientist counted 90,000 nematodes in a single decomposing apple. Roundworms can live almost anywhere, including some of the harshest habitats known—polar ice, hot springs, and the deepest trenches of the ocean.

Roundworms take a heavy toll on agriculture, destroying between 7 and 15 percent of the U.S. food crop, worth billions of dollars, each year. They commonly infect humans as well, causing disease and death.

Yet many people go through life not even knowing that nematodes exist. These small, soft-bodied creatures remain mysterious not only to the average person but to biologists as well. Approximately 15,000 species of nematodes have been described. Most experts agree that this is just a drop in the bucket compared to the numbers that exist. Some estimate that there may be half a million species.

Much of our unfamiliarity with nematodes has to do with their size. Although one parasitic variety found in sperm whales has been measured at 26 feet (8 m) long and 1 inch (2.5 cm) wide, many of them cannot be seen without a miscroscope. Some multi-celled nematodes are even smaller than a few single-celled protozoans.

At least one roundworm has been known to humans for many centuries. A large intestinal parasite called *Ascaris* was described as early as 1550 B.C. But for most of human history, worms were considered worms, and the distinction between flatworms and roundworms was not made until fairly recently. Sorting one nematode from another is a daunting task, even today. Roundworms tend to look so much alike that it is difficult to separate one species from another.

Roundworms pursue much the same food-gathering strategy as the flatworms, and so have a similar body plan. These bilaterally symmetrical animals actively seek out food. Their streamlined, cylindrical shape is better suited than the flatworms' for burrowing and crawling in small openings. Many nematodes are able to crawl through the tiny space between grains of sand. A simple system of muscle contractions provides them with a crawling motion, and, in a few cases, allows them to swim.

As with the flatworms, nematodes have a nervous system concentrated in the front end. A central mass of nerves acts as a sort of brain that controls the body movements and governs the senses. The head end also has small pits known as *amphids* that contain cells that can detect such stimuli as touch and chemicals.

Other similarities to flatworms include the ability to absorb oxygen through their cell membranes, the tendency of numerous species to gain their nutrients from parasitism, and their methods of reproduction.

Like flatworms, sexual reproduction is the preferred,

49

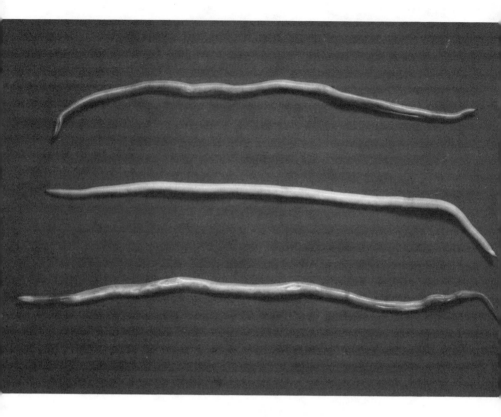

The Ascaris has a streamlined shape ideal for burrowing into small spaces. Roughly one-fourth of the human population is believed to be infested with these worms.

but not the only, method of continuing the species. A few can fertilize their own eggs, and the parasitic forms have a complicated cycle of development that requires different hosts at different stages, as do the parasitic flatworms. Flatworms ensure survival by producing enormous numbers of eggs, and roundworms take a backseat to no animal in flooding the environment with their young. *Ascaris* produce eggs faster than a machine gun fires bullets! A female *Ascaris* is capable of producing between 1 and 3 million eggs a day.

Nematodes have come up with some addditional methods of ensuring survival of their species. They increase the chances of eggs being fertilized by giving off sexual attractants that draw males and females together. One parasite found in a rat's bladder goes a step further to guarantee fertilization. In this species, the male nematode lives inside the much larger female.

Some roundworms, especially parasitic ones, ensure survival of the species in the harshest conditions by means of a highly resistant juvenile stage. The young nematodes appear to be dead and can remain that way for years while waiting for favorable conditions or for the right host to infect. Nematodes can survive for several years in the soil in this virtually lifeless stage, and have even been revived after thirty years of dormancy. When they are placed in water, they revive and continue their development. In contrast to the long-lived juvenile resistant stage, parasitic adults have a short life span. Once they infect their final host, they may die within a matter of weeks.

Although their crawling method of movement does not allow adult nematodes to travel far, nematode eggs are light enough to be blown great distances in the air. Eggs of parasitic roundworms can enter a host by being inhaled, and can then be spread by their host, who passes them into the environment in its feces.

A key difference between flatworms and roundworms is the digestive process. Roundworms are far more diverse in their eating habits. Some nematodes are carnivores who feed on protozoans and worms, some are parasites, some feed on bacteria and decaying plant matter. Others have found ways to tap into growing plants, a food source not available to simpler animals.

This diversity of diet is reflected in the construction

of the mouth, which in roundworms is located in the front. Bacteria eaters have small, simple openings; carnivores may have larger mouths with sharp, toothlike structures; and many plant feeders have a special apparatus called a *stylet*. A stylet is something like a hollow needle that can pierce tough plant walls and suck out the plant juices.

The roundworm's interior includes three layers of cells like the flatworm's, but it follows along the cnidarian pathway of creating an inner environment within a body cavity. This body cavity is not well developed and is mainly filled with fluid. However, it does contain a complete digestive tract, including an intestine. Nematodes appear to be the simplest animals that have solved the problem of eliminating unused food from the body. They pass waste through the entire digestive tract and out the other end through an opening called the *anus*.

A hard outer layer of cells, called a *cuticle*, gives the roundworm some protection against the outside environment. This cuticle is shed, or molted, several times during development, with a new cuticle growing in the old one's place. As they grow, nematodes usually molt four times. The reason for this is not clear, since the cuticle is capable of growing along with the rest of the nematode body and so is not outgrown.

Nematodes are primarily known to humans for the damage they do. Humans can be infected by more than three dozen different species. Trichinosis is a disease that pigs often contract by eating nematode-infected rats. The disease can be transferred to humans who eat raw or undercooked pork. After it is eaten by humans, the immature or larval stage of the *Trichinella* bores a hole through the digestive system walls and goes to the muscles, where it forms a cyst. This causes painful swelling that can sometimes result in death.

Another nematode is responsible for "river blindness," a disease that affects 20 million Africans, causing blindness in about 10 percent of the cases. Guinea worms infect 50 million Asians and Africans each year. Hookworm is one of the world's most widespread health problems, afflicting 400 to 600 million people worldwide. The ground-dwelling hookworm larvae latch onto the human foot, although they often climb a short way up a damp human leg before penetrating the skin. Once the nematodes burrow inside, they bore into the intestines, where they feed on blood. Hookworms cause anemia, weakness, slow mental development, and sometimes death. Hookworm infection can often be prevented simply by wearing shoes.

Nematodes cause other diseases, ranging from the common to the bizarre. Young children throughout the world are often bothered by pinworms that cause itching. A far rarer but more hideous problem is elephantiasis. This disease is caused by *Wuchereria bancrofti*, a small, threadlike nematode that blocks the lymph ducts and causes grotesque swelling. The leg of a person afflicted with elephantiasis can swell to many times its normal diameter.

Nematodes do not limit their parasitism to humans. Heartworms attack dogs. Several species cost farmers millions of dollars by attacking swine and poultry.

In nature, nematodes that feed on plants cause a limited amount of damage. Most restrict their feeding to a particular kind of plant. Since natural communities usually consist of a wide variety of plant species, the impact of a particular nematode on that community is hardly noticeable. Agriculture, however, has provided nematodes with opportunities for feasting. By growing only one kind of plant in a field, farmers leave that field open to wholesale devastation by a single species of nematode.

There are many nematodes ready to take advantage. Potatoes alone attract three dozen species. Other important crops nematodes feed on are wheat, coffee, fruit,

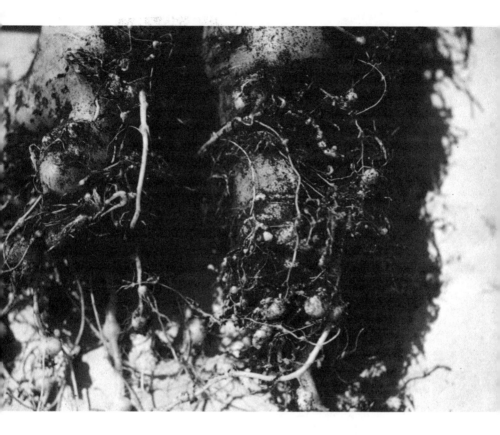

Parasitic nematodes have fed on these carrot roots, causing them to develop knots.

vegetables, cotton, tobacco, and legumes. Nematodes rarely kill plants, but cause damage by removing cytoplasm and by releasing toxins into the plant. The damage caused can take many shapes, including wilted leaves, stunted growth, rot, deformities, galls (lumpy tumors), and poor-quality fruit.

Humans have fought back by rotating crops to remove certain types of plants from a field infested with parasites, by developing crop varieties that resist nematode attack, by poisoning, and by introducing natural enemies to nematode-infested areas.

Despite this long list of destruction, nematodes also produce some benefits. They help to maintain natural balance in the soil, to control insect pests, and they provide an important link in the food chain as prey for mites, annelids, and insects.

6
ANNELIDS: SEGMENTED WORMS

The third phylum of worms, the annelids or "ringed worms," includes the familiar earthworm. On the surface, earthworms appear to be about as primitive as an animal can get. They seem to have no useful features at all—no eyes or other external sense organs, no appendages. The head looks similar to the tail.

Appearances are deceiving, though. The rings around the body for which annelids are named may not look like much, but they divide the worms into flexible segments that give annelids far more mobility than the other worms. In addition, the lowly earthworm has broken through to develop a protected inner environment that simpler animals have not quite managed. Its three layers of cells are organized in such a way that its body cavity is lined on all sides by a thin sheet of cells. This lined body cavity is called a *coelom*, and is found in all the more complex animals, including humans. The coelom contains the digestive tract, as well as other es-

The earthworm's segmented body gives it the
flexibility to twist in many directions at once.

sential organs that perform necessary survival tasks far more efficiently than a collection of cells or tissue.

Annelids cannot begin to match the species success of the nematodes. Somewhere around 12,000 annelids have been described. But they are far more visible than flatworms or roundworms. A person can hardly sink a spade into the ground without uncovering a writhing earthworm. An average acre of ground contains more than a ton of these creatures. Soil rich in decaying matter may hold more than a million worms per acre.

Like nematodes, annelids have found homes in diverse habitats. Unlike the roundworms, annelids come in a wide variety of shapes and sizes. They are divided into three main groups according to their number of bristlelike appendages.

The polychaetes, or "many-bristled" worms, live primarily in the ocean. Each of their segments possesses a pair of parapodia, or sidefeet, to which the bristles are attached. Polychaetes are far more diverse in appearance than other worms. Many of them are colorful, and their parapodia come in a variety of shapes. There are about 8,000 known species, few of which are familiar to the average person. They have such descriptive common names as ragworms, fanworms, fireworms, paddleworms, and lugworms.

Oligochaetes, which include earthworms, have no parapodia and possess only a few bristles, which may be almost invisible to the human eye. These worms can be found in the soil almost everywhere on earth except for deserts. Less conspicuous are the freshwater oligo-

The fireworm, sometimes known as the bristleworm, displays toxic bristles, or setae, that extend from its sides.

chaetes, but they are no less abundant. A square yard of mud on a lake bottom may contain 8,000 inch-and-a-half long *Tubifex* worms. About 3,000 species of oligo-chaetes have been identified, ranging in length from 1 yard (1 m) to 3 yards (3 m).

The order Hirudinea, commonly known as leeches, consists of annelids without bristles. Unlike the other annelids, the 500 or so species of leeches are all para-sitic. These aquatic animals are generally smaller than earthworms. In past centuries, leeches were valued as medical tools. Shortly after the Civil War, more than one and a half million leeches per year were used in the United States to suck out the poisonous body fluids that were believed to cause illness. With the decline in me-dicinal use, leeches' primary significance to humans has been as fish bait.

The segmented body of annelids, in combination with their muscle system, provides them with as much flexibility as any animal in the world. Earthworms are divided into 100 to 200 segments, each marked off by rings in the outer surface. Leeches have 33 internal seg-ments, but may have from three to five outside groves in each segment.

Earthworms have two sets of muscles; one set runs lengthwise down the body, and one circles the body parallel to the rings. The worm moves by first squeezing the circular muscles, which causes the body to become long and thin. Then it holds on to the ground on the front end with its tiny bristles while contracting the longitudi-nal muscles. This pulls the body together, bringing the rear end forward.

Because of the segments, earthworms do not have to contract all of the muscles at once. They can thicken segments in the rear end of the body while stretching out the forward segments. This gives them the ability to twist into almost any position and double back on themselves. Such a means of locomotion is perfect for an animal that lives in cramped underground spaces. Earthworms can work their way through tiny open spaces in the soil without getting stuck. If they encounter danger in close quarters, they can contract quickly to pull themselves back to safety. An earthworm's muscles are also powerful enough to shove aside stones that bar its way. An earthworm is capable of moving objects fifty times its weight, the equivalent of a person moving a 40,000-pound (18,200-kg) object. Sometimes it simply tunnels its way through by swallowing dirt.

A leech is similarly flexible but moves in a slightly different way. It can pull itself along by means of suckers, one on each end of its body. The leech attaches the rear sucker to the hard surface, then reaches out with the front end and attaches that sucker to the surface; it then releases the rear sucker and brings the rear end forward. Many of these worms are also capable of a type of swimming motion.

To direct their complex muscle movements, the annelids require a fairly developed nervous system. Each segment of the earthworm contains a branch of nerves to govern that segment. Typical of bilaterally symmetrical animals, earthworms also have a concentration of nerves near the front end; these make up a small brain. There are no internal walls between segments. This allows the nerve branches in the segments to be connected to the brain by a nerve cord that runs the length of the body. Earthworms have such relatively large nerves that they are often used by researchers interested in measuring the electrical and chemical activity of nerves.

Earthworms have no eyes, nose, ears, or other external sensing devices for gaining information from their environment. Yet they do have receptors, scattered over their bodies, that can detect light. Earthworms will immediately burrow away from any light they detect. Other annelids are better equipped as far as senses. Some polychaetes, for example, have large eyes. African land leeches can detect heat, which allows them to fall from leaves on to animals that pass close by.

Most annelids are predators or scavengers. The predators dine on insect larvae, crustaceans, snails, and smaller worms. Polychaetes are the best suited for capturing prey. Some have powerful jaws, others have tentacles. A few live in burrows and lie in wait for small animals to happen by. Fireworms, found most commonly in the West Indies, deliver a toxin to their prey. This toxin is capable of causing a painful burn to humans.

Leeches obtain nutrients from the blood of other animals. Most latch onto larger animals, pierce the skin, and suck out the blood. By secreting a chemical that prevents blood clotting in the wound, they keep the blood flowing until they have had enough. Leeches are capable of gorging themselves with so much blood at one time that they seldom need to eat. A growing leech could survive on two meals a year. The leech's digestive system concentrates the blood by removing water from it; this way it does not have to carry all that weight around.

Earthworms are primarily scavengers who eat the remains of plants and animals. Their mouths contain a fleshy lobe that helps bring food into the body. Earthworms eat their own weight in food every day and cannot help but swallow large amounts of soil along with the food. They are excellent recyclers who can even consume old rags and paper.

This type of diet requires a series of digestive organs in order to separate usable nutrients from unusable material. The food goes through the esophagus into the crop, where food is stored. There is some indication that digestive enzymes may begin to act on food in the crop. From there the food moves to a gizzard, where it is ground into digestible bits. This material is moved on to the intestines, where it undergoes the final stage of digestion. Earthworm intestines are capable of digesting cellulose, a tough plant fiber that most animals cannot use. Nutrients from the food are then absorbed into the body. Waste material is passed out of the body through the anus and is deposited in small piles called *casts*. Earthworms deposit these casts either on top of the soil or in underground burrows.

An earthworm is large enough so that much of its body lies too far from the intestines to absorb nutrients from it. The earthworm transports nutrients to the far reaches of its body by a network of blood vessels. The blood is circulated by five large vessels near the front end of the worm that pump the blood by contractions.

This blood also acts as a transport system for oxygen and carbon dioxide. Earthworms, like all the simpler animals, obtain oxygen and remove carbon dioxide through direct exchange with the environment. Blood vessels near the surface take up the oxygen that passes through the skin and carry it to cells throughout the body. Carbon dioxide is carried away from internal cells back to the surface. This process requires a moist skin, which is why the worm covers itself with a smooth, slippery substance called *mucus*. Earthworms must stay in moist environments or this mucus will dry out and the worms will suffocate.

Annelids have developed a number of the organs that more complex animals have found useful. Some polychaetes have developed gills to more efficiently pull oxygen from the water. Earthworms contain *nephridia*, organs that function much like kidneys to rid the body of those waste products that result from cell activity rather than from digestion.

Reproduction in annelids is usually sexual. Earthworms and leeches, however, resemble some of the simpler animals in that each individual contains both male and female sex organs. They do not fertilize their eggs with their own sperm but exchange sperm with a mate. Both eggs and sperm are collected by a *clitellum*, a swollen outer ring that is shed over the worm's head. The eggs are then encased in a cocoon, which is either carried for a while, deposited free in the soil, or attached to an object. Unlike their parents, eggs in a cocoon can survive either dry or freezing conditions. They hatch only when conditions are favorable—moist and mild.

Annelids do not expend the enormous amount of energy of roundworms in producing eggs. An earthworm cocoon holds only two to four eggs. But earthworms ensure survival by developing rapidly—they are capable of reproducing at three months of age. Unlike roundworms, annelids have no larval stages or series of hosts to pass through.

Annelids are vital creatures in maintaining the balance of nature. Earthworms in an acre of forest may eat 10 tons of dead plant and animal material, breaking it down into simpler nutrients that can be used by other animals. Their burrowing also aids plant growth by mixing and aerating the soil.

7
MOLLUSKS

With its soft, cylindrical body and lack of appendages, a snail looks like a worm carrying a shell on its back. Based on external appearances, the snail seems more closely related to the worm than to a many-armed squid. The eight-armed octopus seems to have a lot more in common with an eight-legged spider than with a clam. Yet snails, squid, octopus, and clams all belong together in the phylum Mollusca.

Of all the invertebrates, the mollusks have taken on the most widely diverse lifestyles and appearances. Some have adopted the stationary, filter-feeding habits common among the simpler animals. Others have developed complex brains and sensory organs typical of more complex animals. Some swim powerfully in the ocean, some crawl on land. Some have developed specialized organs to breathe in the water; others have organs that allow them to breathe air.

Around 100,000 species of mollusks have been identified, and many extinct species have left their mark in fossil records. Only the insects have more species, and they tend to be more similar to each other than many of the mollusks. Mollusks, one of the dominant groups of the ocean, are common in fresh water and can occasionally be found on land. This forms a pearl.

Mollusks are primarily important to humans as food, the favorites being clams, oysters, scallops, squid, and snails. Oysters are also important because they create beautiful pearls. When particles of sand enter their shells, the sand is coated with a special substance that protects the oysters from irritation.

Mollusks are grouped together because they share a unique body form. They are soft-bodied animals with a head, a foot, and a fold of skin called the *mantle* that contains the internal organs. The mantle's main function appears to be to protect these delicate organs. The many ways in which mollusks have made use of the mantle accounts for the astounding variety of forms.

In most cases, the mantle secretes a substance, composed mostly of calcium carbonate, that hardens into a shell. Shells are the most distinctive physical feature of mollusks, and they come in such a variety of sizes and shapes that they are used as the main means of identifying many mollusk species.

The rigid shell offers mollusks the advantage of protection. Unlike the worms, whose soft bodies lie exposed, many mollusks can retreat into the shell when in danger.

One main disadvantage of shells is that they are not made up of living, dividing cells. That presents the problem of how to keep a developing animal from outgrowing its shell. Many mollusks have solved this problem with a shell design that allows the animal to build on to the shell in a way that can accommodate its increased body size. The shell is not continuously added on to, but is periodically expanded when the need arises.

Shells also have the disadvantage of cutting down on mobility. Except for those mollusks with greatly reduced shells (such as the octopus), most mollusks, like the snail, lumber along under their loads or, like the clam, stay fairly stationary.

The mantle cells can provide other methods of defense for mollusks—an ink cloud that an octopus can squirt to help it hide from an attacker, acids that a sea slug can emit to fight off attack, and a strong aroma that a land snail can exude to discourage potential predators. The clam mantle secretes mucus, which helps it collect food.

Another characteristic of most mollusks is a *radula*, a tonguelike projection of the mouth. The radula is lined with rasping teeth that help the animal obtain food.

The phylum Mollusca contains seven classes, the most important of which are the gastropods, the bivalves, and the cephalopods. Gastropods, the snails and slugs, make up the largest class of mollusks, with more than 60,000 species. Most of these species can be identified by their shells.

Snails can be found in almost all aquatic habitats, with a few species living on land. All of them need calcium carbonate for building their shells, and so are not common in sandy soils where this material is not available. Slugs differ from snails in that they generally have only a small internal shell, if any.

The coiled pattern of the gastropod shell makes it compact and stable. The snail can fit its entire body inside a relatively small shell that is not too cumbersome to carry around on its back.

All gastropods move by sliding on their single foot. Land types secrete a slime to help them glide along the surface. Most of them live off plants and dead organic matter, although a few are carnivorous. Some gastropods obtain food by using their radulas to drill holes in the shells of other mollusks.

The clam, a bivalve mollusk, has a mantle divided into two separate lobes. A clam collects small particles of food from water that is brought in by the beating cilia found on its large gills.

The second-largest mollusk class includes the bivalves—clams, mussels, oysters, scallops, and similar creatures. The nearly 20,000 species in this group have two separate lobes of the mantle, each of which secretes a shell. The animals live sandwiched between these two shells. The shells are hinged on one end and can be opened and closed by muscles on either side of the hinge.

Scallops can move by forcing water out between the two halves of their shell, but most bivalves are largely immobile. Like the sponges and cnidarians, they depend on cilia to create a flow of water that will draw tiny, floating food to them. The water flows through the mantle cavity, where the food is filtered out.

Cephalopods number only 650 species but include some of the more fascinating sea creatures, the squids and octopus. *Cephalopod* means "head foot," and refers to the fact that it has a more highly developed head than other mollusks. Other distinctive cephalopod features are the adaptation of the molluscan foot into arms, and a reduced mantle. The shell is usually small—in the octopus it is a barely noticeable internal plate.

Octopus have a roundish head with eight arms or tentacles attached to it. Squid and cuttlefish have more slender trunks with a visible outer shell, and eight arms plus an extra pair of longer tentacles. All cephalopods are armed with suction cups on their tentacles for capturing prey. In addition, some squid have claws for grasping.

Octopus scuttle along the sea bottom, usually living alone. They prefer to eat crab and shellfish, which they can poison and then break open with their hard beaks. Squid swim in packs in the open water, where they hunt fish. They can move quickly either backward or forward by shooting out a jet of water.

Mollusks have well-developed organs similar to those found in complex animals. This includes the typical digestive tract, with a mouth, digestive organs, and an anus. Nutrients are distributed by blood through a circulation system pumped by a heart. Most mollusks provide a one-way trip for the blood through arteries that carry it to the cells throughout the body. There are no vessels to carry it back. Instead, the blood slowly seeps

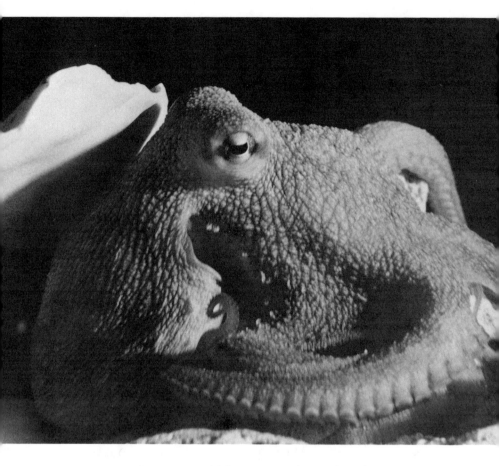

*An octopus hides among the rocks. These
animals are masters of camouflage, and can
change color to blend in with their surroundings.*

back to the heart through small spaces within the body
cavity. Cephalopods have developed a far more efficient
retrieval system, with veins carrying blood back to the
heart.

Mollusks cleanse themselves of the waste products

of metabolism through an excretory system that includes kidneys. Rather than trying to obtain enough oxygen by absorbing it through the skin, mollusks use a more efficient system that makes possible a greater body mass. The aquatic mollusks have gills that take in oxygen from the water and channel it into the blood system. In bivalves, the gills fill a large portion of the mantle cavity. They have also been adapted to filter out food as well as oxygen. Again, the cephalopods have developed the most efficient gill system. The greater amount of oxygen they can absorb allows them to lead a far more active life than other mollusks. Land snails and slugs have lungs that take in oxygen from the air.

The complexity of the nervous system depends on the lifestyle of the animal. Bivalves, being stationary creatures, meet the environment equally on all sides and have no need for a concentration of sensory equipment on the forward end. Like the sponges, they have no head. Their nervous system consists of ganglia linked by connecting nerves spread throughout the body. Most mollusks appear to be able to sense both touch and light. The forward-moving snails have nerves concentrated on the forward end. Their light-sensitive equipment is a pair of tentacles that project from the head into the environment. Lower tentacles on a land snail are capable of feeling and alert the animal to what is ahead.

Octopuses are faced with the task of coordinating eight independent arms with a large body that has no external skeleton for support. They are also equipped with a number of devices for gaining information from the environment. The powerful spherical lenses in their eyes can shift positions to bring objects into focus. Sensors on octopuses' tentacles can feel the difference between different textures and shapes. Octopuses also have a sense of smell.

The octopus could not coordinate its movements or process all this information without a centralized nervous command center. Its brain is the most highly developed among all invertebrates, with especially large vision and smell lobes. The octopus brain is capable of performing complicated tasks that require memory and learning.

Mollusks reproduce sexually but display reproductive adaptations that are as varied as their body forms. Most gastropods have both male and female sexual organs. Other mollusks are generally either male or female, yet there are some bizarre exceptions within the phylum. *Crepidula* snails, which prefer to live together stacked one upon another, are usually one sex or the other. But if a male is removed from the stack and separated from females, it will become female. The quahog clam of the Atlantic begins life as a male, then becomes female, which it stays for the rest of its life. Some female clams, after spawning, go back to being male again.

Molluscan young hatch from eggs. Clams and snails are usually protected from the time of their hatching by a tiny shell. Unlike the simpler animals, the octopus parent takes an active interest in caring for its eggs. It fastens its eggs to rocks, then stands guard over them for weeks until they hatch. Octopus mothers sometimes spray the eggs with a stream of water to clean them of debris.

Even those mollusks with advanced sensing systems are not without enemies. The octopus is preyed upon by the moray eel, the giant squid is eaten by whales, and other mollusks make up the diet of birds and starfish. But generally, they are well adapted to the ocean, as their abundance of species shows.

Their body plan, though, does not lend itself well to life on land, where their lack of mobility presents a great problem. That still leaves the land habitat very much available for an animal that can develop some means of moving quickly from place to place.

8
ARTHROPODS PART 1: CRUSTACEANS AND ARACHNIDS

Humans have found great advantages in being able to travel long distances quickly. The quest for mobility has taken us from horseback and carriages to automobiles and jets.

Mobility is just as advantageous to invertebrates, and the group that has developed the most along these lines has been by far the most successful. The arthropods include more than a million species, about three-fourths of the animal species on earth. *Arthropod* means "jointed limb," and this physical feature has helped two groups of arthropods overrun the land environments. A leg with joints that bend has the flexibility needed to produce rapid movement. In arthropods, the jointed limbs occur in pairs, which work in tandem to produce even more rapid movement.

By themselves, jointed limbs would be of little use. The muscle structure required to move the limbs needs to be attached to a strong framework. Arthropods provide that framework in the form of a hard, external skeleton.

73

Unlike mollusk shells, which are composed mainly of calcium carbonate, arthropod shells contain a chemical compound known as *chitin*. This material is more flexible than calcium carbonate. It can be molded into a variety of shapes and is less cumbersome to carry around. The chitinous shell provides the same support as a mollusk shell but does not restrict the animal's mobility. In order to get these advantages, arthropods sacrifice a measure of safety. While mollusks are able to add on to their existing shells, arthropods can retain their flexibility only by molting their exoskeletons and growing new ones. Arthropods must do this several times during their growth stages; each time they are vulnerable while their new skeleton is forming.

Another characteristic of arthropods is a segmented body, a feature seen before in the annelids. Arthropod segments are larger and more efficient than annelid segments. One of the arthropod segments is a distinct head containing a relatively large brain. This brain controls a nervous system constructed along the same lines as the annelids', only more complex so that it can coordinate greater muscular movements and more intricate sense detection. Most arthropods have compound eyes made up of many lenses, each of which focuses on the area directly in front of it.

Arthropods generally have a simple circulation system with a limited number of blood vessels. The body cavity has been reduced and is filled with a pool of blood that surrounds the organs. The blood is moved around, in most cases, by the pumping action of a heart, although some arthropods can circulate blood only by the movement of their bodies.

In the past, all the animals that shared arthropod characteristics were grouped into a single phylum. This included three main groups: crustaceans, arachnids, and insects. More recently, some experts have come to believe that these groups are not closely related after all, but that they have evolved their similar characteristics independently and should be placed in different categories.

Crustaceans, with the exception of wood lice, live in water. This group contains 25,000 identified species that include lobsters, crabs, shrimp, crayfish, and many tiny aquatic animals. The typical crustacean has two pairs of sensory antennae and five pairs of appendages. In many of the larger crustaceans, the forward pair of appendages has evolved into food-grasping pincers.

Along with the familiar commercial seafood species, crustaceans include tiny creatures called copepods. Although only a few millimeters long, these are some of the most important animals in the marine food chain. Copepods make up a large part of the plankton that is the major food source for other crustaceans, mollusks, and fish such as herring and mackerel. Copepods hunt protozoans during most of the year. But when the plant plankton blooms in the spring, they become filter-feeders. Copepods pull in a current of water with their antennae that can beat at the rate of 1,000 strokes per minute; this helps them to filter out the tiny plants. Krill are a larger form of crustacean plankton eaten by whales.

Most other crustaceans are active predators, like shrimp who feed on copepods, or scavenging carnivores, such as lobsters who live off dead or living animals they find on rocky ocean bottoms. A few, such as crayfish, will eat both plants and animals. Barnacles are an exception. They have adopted the filter-feeding lifestyle, attaching themselves to rocks or objects such as boat bottoms. This has made them a nuisance to humans. A single year's growth of barnacles puts such a drag on a boat that it can increase fuel costs by 40 percent.

Crustaceans gain oxygen in different ways depending upon their size. Crustacean plankton are small enough that their cells can absorb oxygen directly from the water. In larger animals, such as the lobster, which can grow to nearly 50 pounds (23 kg), a more efficient means is needed. These animals have feathery gills to extract oxygen from the water. The gills are lined with blood vessels that transport the oxygen to other areas of the body. The terrestrial wood lice, commonly known as pill bugs, have a type of gill that is covered with a thin film of water. This enables them to use their gills to absorb oxygen from the air. Despite living on land, these creatures must stay moist or they will lose their ability to gain oxygen. A few species of wood lice have developed air-breathing tubes in their bodies as an adaptation to life on land.

Crustaceans reproduce sexually and develop through a series of larval stages. Generally, the young are left to survive on their own, although female lobsters carry their fertilized eggs beneath their abdomen until they are ready to hatch. Freshwater fairy shrimp have increased their species' chances of survival by developing especially resistant eggs to help the eggs survive dry times. In fact, they must be gotten wet more than once before they will hatch.

In addition to their tough shells, crustaceans have developed several means of defense. Lobsters can defend themselves with their pincers. Crabs can run quickly. Some species of crabs can burrow into the sand in a flash; others cover themselves with plants and sponges

This female lobster's eggs will be carried right below her abdomen until they are ready to hatch.

Lobsters have one large pincer for crushing objects and a smaller one for holding and tearing.

as camouflage. Hermit crabs take over the shells of dead mollusks as protection. They have highly developed senses of sight and touch that enable them to rummage among the shells and choose one that fits them perfectly.

A highly developed sense of sight also characterizes another group, the arachnids. This group includes spiders, scorpions, harvestmen (daddy longlegs), and ticks, all of which have four pairs of legs and a body divided into two main sections.

Most of the 70,000 species of arachnids have adapted the arthropod body form to dry land. The main difficulties with living on land are the greater need for body support, the danger of drying up in the absence of water, the need for a way to obtain oxygen from the air rather than from water, and the need for an efficient method of locomotion to cover the greater distances between food and water.

Many sea creatures, the best example being the jellyfish, use the buoyancy of water to give them form and support. The atmosphere is not dense enough to provide that kind of support, so land creatures need a built-in framework. The rigid yet versatile exoskeleton made of chitin gives arachnids a solid structure. It combines with muscles and jointed limbs to give spiders great mobility. The chitinous armor further helps the arachnids adapt to land life by being waterproof. This prevents vital body fluids from evaporating.

Spiders do not require a moist skin to draw in oxygen. Instead, they gather that vital element through special respiratory organs known as book lungs, which are located on the abdomen. Book lungs are fine plates of tissue richly supplied with blood. They can pull oxygen out of the air and transfer it to the blood, which then circulates it to the cells.

Another problem land-dwelling creatures overcome is freezing temperatures. Spiders have responded to this challenge by developing glycoprotein compounds that inhibit freezing.

As bilaterally symmetrical, forward-moving hunters, arachnids have sense detectors on their front end to give them information about what lies ahead. They sense their environment with two projections called palps, located near the head. Arachnids also usually have six or eight pairs of eyes to help them detect objects or animals well in advance of actually encountering them.

Almost all spiders are predators. Some, such as wolf spiders and jumping spiders, use their sense of sight to stalk and hunt down prey, which usually consists of insects. Others rely more on their palps to feel the identity of their prey. Those that do not actively pursue prey have developed the food-gathering behavior of setting traps. Some of the traps are quite simple. Crab spiders commonly hide among plants and ambush insects that come to feed. Other spiders build webs, ranging from a few haphazard strands to elaborate and intricately designed orbs.

Web weaving is not learned behavior, but rather is inborn knowledge called *instinct*. A young spiderling spinning its first web can spin as beautiful a design as an older spider. Webs are made from a liquid silk produced in glands of the abdomen and shot out through spinnerets at the rear of the body. The liquid hardens on contact with the air to form the strands of the web. These strands are so thin that they are almost invisible to their prey and can be easily blundered into. Sticky threads produced in a different gland are added to the web to ensnare the victim.

Spiders wait in hiding for an insect to get tangled in their trap. They stay in contact with their trap by a thread that acts like a fishing bobber. The vibration tells them when they have caught something and the spider scurries out to inspect its catch. The spider's feet are coated with

an oily film that prevents it from getting stuck in its own web. Spiders are able to distinguish edible prey from more dangerous creatures who may have wandered into their trap. If a wasp gets caught in the web, the spider may simply cut enough lines to let it escape.

If the prey is easily manageable, the spider bites it and injects a poison that immobilizes or kills it. Then it wraps the insect in fresh silk and saves it for a later meal.

Another group of land-dwelling arachnids are the scorpions. These creatures do not spin webs. They look more like small crustaceans than spiders, complete with large forward pincers and a tail. Most have adapted to living in very dry climates and to hunting at night.

The scorpion's tail is tipped with a stinger that may contain a powerful venom. This stinger is used more for defense than for killing prey, however. Scorpions can usually subdue their prey (spiders, grasshoppers, beetles, and other insects) by grasping them with their pincers. Like spiders, scorpions consume only the juices of their prey. Ticks, another group of arachnids, burrow their heads through the skin to feed on blood and have enough storage capacity to ingest 200 times their own weight in blood at a single feeding.

Perhaps the most unusual aspect of arachnids is their reproduction method. Spiders readily eat other spiders, even of their own species. This makes mating a risky proposition, especially for the males, who are usually much smaller. Many female spiders eat the male immediately after mating with him.

Males have developed many different behaviors to counteract this danger. Many of them engage in a court-

This spider has successfully trapped a meal in the sticky threads of its web.

ship dance. This could be a way of attracting the female's attention from a safe distance, or a test to help the male determine the female's intentions, or even a safe way of helping the female to distinguish between a mate and an ordinary meal. Some males play it even safer, staying back and plucking the strands of the web to alert the female to the possibility of mating.

In some species, to keep from being poisoned the male locks fangs with the female during mating. Males of another species tie the female in silk before mating. Still other species avoid being eaten by presenting the female with a silk-wrapped insect meal.

Spiders that have mated then lay eggs in silken cocoons. Some spiders show maternal behavior in that the female carries the cocoon with her and occasionally puts it in the sun to warm. Other spiders hide their cocoons in vegetation.

9
ARTHROPODS PART 2: INSECTS

~~~~~~~~~~~~~~~~~~~~~~~~~~~~~~~~

Although spiders are well adapted to the terrestrial environment, they have been far surpassed by the insects.
Insects have so overrun the land regions of the earth that
no one knows how many species exist. A million insect
species, making up well over two-thirds of all known
animal species, have been identified. A single order of
insects, the beetles, number more than 300,000 species,
far more than any other phylum.

Insects differ from spiders in that they have only three
pairs of legs rather than four, and three clearly divided
main body segments—the head, thorax, and abdomen.

Insects have used the arthropod form to adjust to
land in much the same way as the arachnids. They rely
on the chitinous exoskeleton for stability and protection
and on the jointed appendages for mobility.

Instead of gills or book lungs, however, insects
breathe through a vast maze of tiny tubes called *tracheae*. Through movements of the abdomen, insects

draw in air through pores in the body called *spiracles* that branch into the tracheae. Since no cell is far from one of these tubes, insects do not need to distribute oxygen through the circulatory system. Cells absorb it directly from the tracheae. This system has some disadvantages. Air travels slowly through the tubes, especially at colder temperatures when the air is denser.

The relative inefficiency of the trachea system in obtaining oxygen is one reason insects are so small, generally weighing less than an ounce. Insects are also restricted by the weight of the exoskeleton and by the problem of retaining moisture. They have a large surface-to-volume ratio. While that is an advantage to animals that diffuse oxygen from water, it presents a major problem for an animal trying to retain moisture. Many insects decrease evaporation by secreting a waxy substance on their outer surfaces. The largest insects live in the tropics, where the air is warm enough to allow greater flow through the trachea and humid enough to keep evaporation to a minimum.

Without the need of blood for oxygen transport, the insects' circulation system has remained fairly simple. It is largely an open blood system with few vessels. Liquid wastes are dealt with through a more elaborate system of Malpigian tubes, which function like kidneys in removing waste from the blood.

The overwhelming success of insects on land can be attributed to adaptations in three areas: eating mechanisms, senses, and mobility.

Although land plants provide a rich store of nutrients, most animals are not able to make use of the vast majority of them. Land plants are often made up of large amounts of tough structural material in the form of cellulose and lignin. Most animals are not able to digest this. Plants have also developed many protective substances such as toxins and unpleasant odors, and physical barriers such as thorns and shells.

Insects have been by far the most successful group of animals in getting past these barriers. They have developed an arsenal of specialized mouth structures and digestive systems that attack virtually any plant in existence. In addition, insects have broadened their tastes to feed off a great variety of food sources, from other insects to worms, rotting meat, flakes of dead skin, animal waste, and human blood. Some types of insects, such as cockroaches and house crickets, will eat almost anything they find.

Insect mouths are highly specialized to exploit the particular food source favored by the species. Ants, beetles, cockroaches, dragonflies, and grasshoppers all have hard external mouthparts for biting through and breaking up tough material. Jawlike structures called *mandibles* are much larger in the meat-eating insects such as ground beetles than in the leaf-clipping grasshoppers. The lower lip of the dragonfly has sharp pincers on the end that can be shot out to capture prey.

Many other insects have mouths adapted to obtain food by sucking. Some of these, such as aphids, butterflies, and moths, feed on the juices of plants. Butterflies unroll their tongues and insert them into flowers to suck up the nectar. Aphids have a long, needlelike drill that pierces through the hard plant exterior, and special muscles for pumping out the sap. Many forms attack the stems, where the sap flows under such high pressure that they hardly need to suck. Female mosquitoes use a similar sucking tube to pierce animal skin and suck out blood. The common housefly also sucks up liquid but does not have a piercing instrument. Instead it laps up surface liquids. Some kinds of bees have it both ways, with sucking mouths for getting nectar from flowers and jaws capable of cutting leaves.

The life cycle of the butterfly best illustrates the amazing adaptability of the insect mouth. During its immature, or larval, stage, the butterfly is a leaf-eating grub

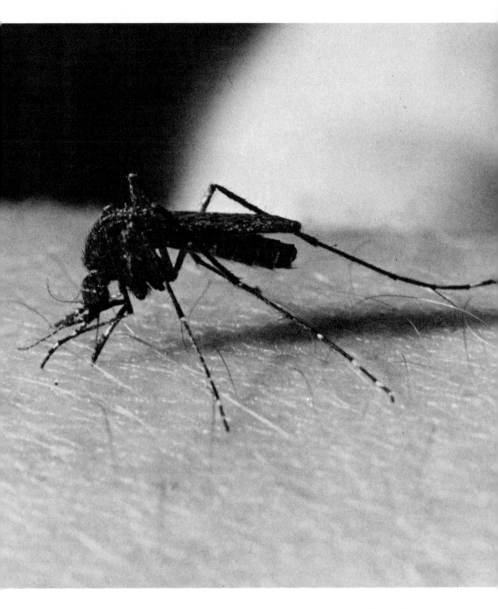

A mosquito sucks blood from a human arm through its hollow tube. This female mosquito must find a meal of blood so that its eggs can develop.

with biting jaws. By the time it completes its transformation into an adult, its mouth has changed into a sap-sucking apparatus.

Insects have adapted in other ways to take advantage of different food sources. Mantids are predators that blend in well with their surroundings. This allows them to pounce on unsuspecting insects, which they grab with their greatly enlarged forelegs. A number of insects have the ability to work together as a community, with each group assigned a specific task. This specialization helps them to accomplish tasks more efficiently. Bees are so highly organized along these lines that workers, drones, and queens are each given a different diet suited to their particular needs. Swarms of biting army ants numbering in the millions can work together to bring down prey many times their size.

Some insects cooperate with other species to tap into food sources. Woodeaters such as termites possess strong jaws to break off and swallow wood. This material would normally be too tough even for an insect to digest. Termites, however, house protozoans in their digestive tract; the protozoans can break down the cellulose and make nutrients available to the mite.

A large measure of insects' survival ability has been due to the development of their senses. Insect senses are coordinated by a brain in the head connected to a series of ganglia that form a central nerve cord.

Most insect bodies are covered with sensitive hairs especially concentrated on the lower legs and the head—the parts most likely to come in contact with the environment. These sensing hairs are able to detect chemicals through smell and taste, and are sensitive to touch. As with the mouth parts, insects display a wide variety of sense adaptations for different purposes. Ants use their antennae to recognize other creatures. They are able to detect the difference, probably through smell, between an ant of their own colony and a foreign ant.

Beetles use their sense of smell to locate decaying carcasses on which to feed. Other insects monitor the more pleasant aromas of flowers to guide them to nectar. Cockroaches thrive in dark places and so depend on their extremely long antennae to provide information on their surroundings. Insects also rely on their sense of smell to help them locate others of their species for reproduction. Moths can detect the scent of a mate at a distance of 2 miles (3.2 km).

Some insects depend more on sight than on smell. A dragonfly, which hunts in the open air, has very short antennae but has a head that seems to be taken up almost entirely by its giant eyes. Insect eyes are not capable of changing focus. They make up for this with compound eyes made up of a number of lenses, each capable of focusing on a small space directly in front of them. Dragonflies can have as many as 30,000 different lenses. This gives them the ability to scan a wide area at once and makes it almost impossible for anything to sneak up on them. The mantis is another hunter with good eyesight.

Moths do not have good vision, which can be an enormous handicap for an airborne creature. Unlike surface dwellers who are always in contact with the ground, flying insects need some kind of sensing device to tell them which direction is up. Moths are sensitive to light and use sunlight as their means of orientation. They are often seen fluttering around fires and light bulbs because these bright lights confuse them and make it hard for them to get their bearings.

Some insects take advantage of another sense not commonly associated with simpler animals—hearing. Mosquitoes can pick up sounds with their antennae. Crickets and grasshoppers hear through special membranes similar to ears. Crickets have these on their forelegs, while in some types of grasshopper they are located on the abdomen. Crickets and grasshoppers make chirping noises by rubbing the edge of their enlarged leg on their forewing. These noises serve largely as sexual attractants.

A third crucial ingredient to insect success has been mobility. Insects can travel great distances quickly regardless of the terrain because of their wings, a feature available to no other invertebrate. Insect wings are not adaptations of legs but are separate appendages made of thin sheets of chitin held together by hollow veins. Butterfly wings are also covered with overlapping scales that give them their distinctive colors and patterns.

The opportunistic insects have adapted the wing for use in many ways. Long-distance fliers, such as dragonflies and moths, have two pairs of wings. The stiff-winged dragonflies are capable of flying over 18 miles (30 km) an hour. Moth wings are sturdy enough to stand up to marathon migrations, yet can be folded so that the moth is less visible to predators.

Flies and mosquitoes have a single pair of wings. They can perform impressive flying feats such as high-speed getaways, hovering in one spot, and taking off in any direction, including backward.

Wings are controlled by special tissues called *fibrillar muscles* that can contract and relax faster than the muscles of any other animal. The fibrillar muscles are automatically geared to beat at a particular speed and so do not require separate nerve impulses to fire each contraction.

Insects also have limbs specially adapted for speed and maneuverability. Beetles and cockroaches use their long legs to run quickly. Grasshoppers have enlarged hind legs that enable them to jump twenty times their length. Aquatic insects are equipped with long legs lined with hairs that act like oars to push them through the water. The houseflies' feet are fitted with cushions that allow them to land safely at high speeds and to even walk upside down on ceilings.

The extreme changes in climate found in many land

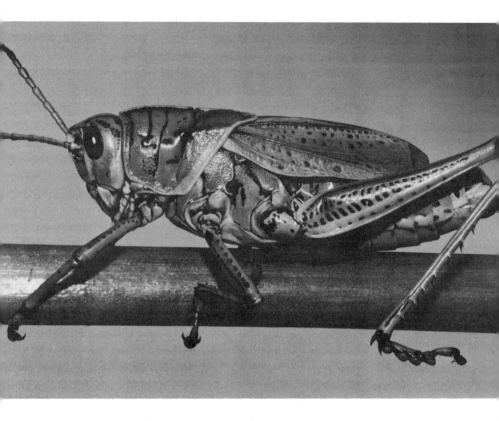

The enlarged hind legs of the grasshopper allow the insect to jump distances many times its body length.

environments pose a threat to insect survival, but insects have developed a number of strategies to cope with them. The gift of flight allows certain insects to migrate thousands of miles to more favorable climates when a change of seasons brings harsh weather. Butterflies combat cold temperatures by gradually collecting a high concentration of glycerol in their bodies; the glycerol acts as a natural antifreeze.

Insects ensure the survival of their species through

rapid sexual reproduction and a multi-stage life cycle. Unlike other arthropods, immature insects may bear little resemblance to adults. Often, they do not even share the same habitat—adult insects generally live on land and the larvae commonly live in water. Some of the more social insects, such as ants and bees, provide a great deal of care for their young. Others, such as flies, may drop their eggs on the ground at random.

In many cases, the insect spends most of its life as a larva and appears only briefly as an adult. Immature dragonflies live from two to four years in their aquatic larval stage and only one year as an adult. Mayflies and cicadas carry this trend to the extreme. The mayfly larvae feed for two or three years on lake bottoms before hatching into adults. They remain adults just long enough to reproduce and die. Adult mayflies do not eat (in fact, they do not even have a digestive tract), and in some cases their adult life span is only a matter of hours. Cicada larvae live underground, feeding on roots, for seventeen years before emerging into a brief adult life.

Social insects such as ants and bees tend to live much longer than other insect species. A queen ant can live for twenty years, producing several million eggs during that time.

Butterflies and moths go through a three-stage life cycle that begins as crawling, wormlike larvae. After a period of voracious eating and rapid growth, the creatures encase themselves in cocoons, or silk pads, and stop all activity. During this inactive or pupal stage, the insects break down the larval structure and transform themselves into adults.

Insects produce many useful products for humans, such as honey, beeswax, silk, and shellac. Even more important is the role they play in pollinating plants and feeding on pest species. But these benefits are usually dwarfed by their negative effects. The role of the mosquito in transmitting malaria, of the locust in destroying

food crops, of the bark beetle in ravaging elm trees, not to mention the sheer nuisance of cockroaches and termites in the home, and mosquitoes and flies in the outdoors, has made insects a prime target of human eradication plans.

The war on insects, however, has not put a dent in that group's drive to populate the earth. Insects are so numerous and adaptable to changing conditions that they can dodge virtually any defense put up against them. They have long shown the ability to develop resistance to toxins and odors developed by plants as defenses. Recently, they have demonstrated the same ability to develop resistance to pesticides. If environmental catastrophe—pollution, toxins, atomic war, or climatic changes—ever overtakes the earth, insects will be far better positioned than humans to survive it.

This butterfly is emerging
from its cocoon stage,
wondrously transformed
from an unsightly grub
into a colorful beauty.

10
ECHINODERMS
~~~~~~~~~~~~~~~~~~~~~~

Although echinoderms are far from the most complex invertebrates, they are tagged on to the end because they are like the leftover pieces of the jigsaw puzzle that do not seem to fit with the rest of the picture.

This exclusively marine phylum contains only 6,000 species, none of which are commercially important. They can be found on the bottom of the ocean nearly anywhere—from the polar seas to the tropics, from tidal beaches to the deepest trenches.

Most echinoderms are easily distinguished by their star-shaped body construction. This flattened, five-pointed design doesn't follow the tendency of animals toward bilateral symmetry. The advantage of this head-less configuration is not clear. Some echinoderms are stationary filter-feeders and so do not require a forward end and a head, but others are predators who seek out their prey. To further confuse the issue, echinoderm larva are bilaterally symmetrical, with a distinct front and rear end.

Typical of animals with no distinct head, echinoderm nerves are not concentrated into anything resembling a brain. These animals maintain contact with their environment by means of widespread receptors that respond to touch and to chemicals, and are distributed evenly throughout the body.

Echinoderms do have a nerve cord that runs along the axis of each arm to coordinate muscle movement. This connecting cord ensures that all the arms move in the same direction when a starfish walks, and gets the muscles to work together to pry open mussel shells. When this cord is cut, each arm walks independently, to the point where starfish may be torn apart by arms going in different directions.

The basic nervous system and lack of a brain appears to put echinoderms among the very simple animals. Yet this group has structures more typical of complex animals. Echinoderms have three layers of body cells and a coelom, or body cavity. They also have a skeleton that is more flexible than that of mollusks or arthropods. The name *echinoderm*, which means "spiny skin," refers to a unique internal skeleton made up of calcium carbonate, the same substance used by mollusks. Rather than building an unwieldy shell to surround their bodies, however, echinoderms build the shell *into* their bodies. Hard nodules of calcium carbonate known as *ossicles* are embedded in the body walls and are surrounded by living tissue. In some species, the nodules stick up like spines.

By spreading the protective shell among the living tissue, echinoderms enjoy the strength and protection of a mollusk shell at a fraction of the weight. They also maintain flexibility. The armored appendages of a starfish can bend easily, while the armored portions of mollusks and arthropods cannot.

Echinoderms have developed a unique circulation system that operates primarily in seawater. This water vascular system consists of a network of canals that run throughout the body. The water in these canals transports food and oxygen to the body cells and carries away carbon dioxide and other waste materials. This system handles the functions of both blood vessels and an excretory system.

The canals are connected to the tube feet that line the bottom surface of the starfish. Some echinoderms are equipped with suckers on these feet. Tube feet are useful in food gathering and oxygen–carbon dioxide exchange, and their coordinated movement helps the animal to crawl along the ocean bottom.

The skin of echinoderms is very thin so that oxygen can diffuse through it. The animals supplement this diffusion with tiny skin gills that stick out from the surface of the skin. Tiny pincers clear sand and grit out of the skin gills so that they are always in contact with water.

Some echinoderms, including most of the extinct species found in fossils, gather food in the filter-feeding manner of the simpler animals. They often resemble sponges in that they are stationary, do not have an anus, and have cilia that create a water current to funnel food toward the mouth, which is generally located on the bottom surface. Some species create no current, but simply collect food that happens by. They "fish" in the water with their tube feet, which are covered with mucus. This mucus traps small food particles and directs them to the mouth. Some species are scavengers. The sand dollars, who have a much more rigid skeleton than starfish, lie half buried in the sand and use their spines and tube feet to collect particles of dead organisms. Sea cucumbers can be found in the pitch dark of the ocean's deepest trenches, where they eat the remains of animals that sink to the bottom. Other echinoderms, such as sea urchins, feed on plants like algae.

Some echinoderms are active predators. Because they move so slowly, their prey is restricted to even slower-moving or stationary animals such as oysters, snails, coral, worms, and other echinoderms. Predatory starfish are drawn to their prey by chemical scents. The long-armed brittle stars are equipped with muscles that allow them to reach out and grab prey. Starfish often latch onto or smother their prey, ingesting whole smaller animals such as gastropods.

One group of starfish, the *Asterias*, has perfected a way to get past the defenses of bivalves, which lock themselves inside their shell when threatened. These echinoderms climb on to the bivalve and attach some of their suckered tube feet to each half of the shell. The arms then pull the two halves of the shell in different directions. Although the starfish is not strong enough to wrench open the shell, the pressure of the tube feet can outlast the muscles holding the shell shut. Eventually, the prey tires. The bivalve muscle has to relax only enough to create a small crack; this allows the starfish to slip some of its stomach folds into the opening. Starfish can digest their prey right in the shell. They are such efficient predators of bivalves that they are a constant threat to commercial oyster beds.

Echinoderms generally are one sex or the other, but individuals of a few species have both male and female organs. Although they usually reproduce sexually, they can also reproduce asexually by regeneration of parts. One of the advantages of a headless body is that no one portion is crucial to the survival of the being; if a starfish is cut into pieces, many of the pieces can grow into a whole animal. Fertilization for sexual reproduction is done outside the body. This might seem hit-or-miss considering the size of the ocean, but such things as water temperature and chemical stimulation cause starfish to release sperm and eggs at the same time. The fertilized eggs grow into larvae, which drift among the oceanic plankton until they develop into adults.

The peculiarities of the echinoderm group cause many experts to wonder if these animals should really

Draped around the clam, this starfish is prying
apart the two halves of the clam's shell by
using its suckered tube feet. If the starfish
gains an opening as small as .1 millimeter, it
can begin to digest the clam right in the shell.

be classified with the invertebrates. Although they do not have backbones, their larvae appear to have much in common with a wormlike ancestor of the vertebrates. Also, the ossicles of the brittle star fit together much like the vertebrae of a backbone. There are far fewer echinoderms today than exist in fossil records, which may indicate that this group is left over from a branch of animal evolution that did not prove to be particularly successful.

GLOSSARY

Asymmetrical. Having no balanced proportions; irregularly shaped.

Bilateral symmetry. A body shape in which the right side is a mirror image of the left side.

Budding. A reproductive method in which a growth on the body of the parent separates from the parent and becomes a new organism.

Calcium carbonate. A salt commonly found in seawater.

Cell fission. The process of cell reproduction in which a single cell splits into two cells.

Cellulose. A tough structural material found in the cell walls of land plants.

Cephalization. The tendency to concentrate sense organs in the forward end so that the animal has a distinct head.

Chitin. A nonliving chemical compound that forms the hard exoskeleton of arthropods.

Chlorophyll. The green pigment in plants that absorbs the light energy plants need to grow.

Choanocytes. The cells lining the inner surface of a sponge wall.

Cilia. The tiny hairs on organisms; these can produce a current or locomotion in water.

Clitellum. The swollen outer ring in annelids in which cocoons are formed.

Cnidoblast. The specialized nerve cells in cnidarians.

Colonies. Groups of individual organisms that function together as one unit.

Cuticle. The hard outer layer of cells.

Fibrillar muscles. The special muscles whose contractions are extremely rapid and, rather than being controlled voluntarily, are set to beat at a particular speed.

Fission. See *cell fission*.

Flagella. Whiplike hairs, longer and less numerous than cilia, used for locomotion and creating currents.

Flame cells. The specialized cells in planarians that filter waste from body fluids.

Food vacuole. A small cavity within a cell in which food particles are broken down into simpler, more usable forms.

Ganglia. Nodules of concentrated nerves.

Gemmule. A small internal bud that is especially resistant to unfavorable environmental conditions.

Genera. The plural of *genus*; divisions in the classification of living things that include members of similar species.

Lignin. The tough, complex material found in the cell walls of many land plants.

Malphigian tubes. The long vessels found in most insects that remove waste from the blood.

Mandible. A hard mouth structure designed to hold or bite food.

Mantle. The fold of skin in mollusks that contains the internal organs.

Medusa. A cnidarian form that floats or swims in the water in the shape of a bell or umbrella.

Mesoglea. A jellylike substance between the external and internal layers of cells, particularly in cnidarians.

Mitochondria. The organelles that convert food molecules and oxygen into energy.

Nematocyst. The stinging cell contained within the cnidoblast.

Nephridia. Organs for removing body waste; found in earthworms.

Organelle. The specialized part of a cell that performs a function similar to the organs of multi-celled creatures.

Osculum. The large opening in sponges for expelling water.

Ossicles. Small, hard nodules of calcium carbonate.

Parapodia. Small appendages protruding from the side of the body, especially in polychaetes.

Parasites. Organisms that obtain their nutrients from the bodies of other living organisms.

Photosynthesis. The process by which a plant uses light to produce vital chemical compounds.

Phylum. One of the major divisions in the classification of living things in the animal kingdom.

Plankton. A broad group of tiny, often microscopic, plants and animals that float in the ocean.

Polyp. A cnidarian form consisting of a plantlike stalk attached to a surface.

Protoplasm. The liquid substance contained within the cell membranes.

Pseudopods. False feet; usually refers to extensions of the amoeba cell.

Radial symmetry. A body shape in which no matter where the animal is cut in half along a single plane, the two sides will be alike.

Radula. A tonguelike projection of the mouth, often lined with rasping teeth that help in obtaining food.

Scavengers. Animals who do not kill their food but rather eat the remains of dead plants and animals.

Schistosomiasis. A disease caused by flatworms; it results in blood loss and tissue damage.

Scolex. The specialized head of a cestode; it has hooks or suckers that latch on to its host.

Species. The final category in biological classification that includes only those living things that share very similar characteristics.

Spicules. Long, sharp supportive structures.

Spongin. The protein that makes up the flexible, elastic structures of sponges.

Stylet. A thin, sharp, piercing tube through which liquids can be drawn.

Surface-to-volume ratio. The number of cells that are exposed to the surface compared to the total number of cells that make up the organism.

Tidal zones. Areas of the ocean that are sometimes underwater and at other times are exposed to the air; this depends on the tides.

Tracheae. The plural of *trachea*; the maze of tubes through which insects draw oxygen.

Trichinosis. A disease produced by roundworms; it results in swelling, pain, and fever.

Tube feet. The small, flexible extensions that line the bottom surface of many echinoderms.

Vacuole. See *food vacuole*.

BIBLIOGRAPHY

Alexander, R. McNeill. *The Invertebrates*. Cambridge: Cambridge University Press, 1979.

Bannister, Keith, and Andrew Campbell. *The Encyclopedia of Aquatic Life*. New York: Facts on File, 1985.

Chinery, Michael, ed. *Dictionary of Animals*. New York: Arco, 1984.

Coldrey, Jennifer. *Discovering Worms*. New York: Bookwright Press, 1986.

Dales, R. P., ed. *Practical Invertebrate Zoology*. Oxford: Blackwell, 1981.

Despommier, Dickson D., and John W. Karapelou. *Parasitic Life Cycles*. New York: Springer-Verlag, 1987.

Farrand, John, Jr., ed. *The Audubon Society Encyclopedia of Animal Life*. New York: Clarkson Potter, 1982.

Line, Les, and Lorus and Margery Milne. *The Audubon Society Book of Insects*. New York: Abrams, 1983.

Najarian, Haig Hagup. *Sex Lives of Animals Without Backbones*. New York: Scribners, 1976.

Parker, Steve. *Seashore*. New York: Knopf, 1989.

Patent, Dorothy Hinshaw. *The World of Worms*. New York: Holiday House, 1978.

Roessler, Carl. *Coral Kingdoms*. New York: Abrams, 1986.

Shale, David, and Jennifer Coldrey. *The Man-of-War at Sea*. Milwaukee: Gareth Stevens, 1987.

Wooten, Anthony. *Insects of the World*. New York: Facts on File, 1984.

INDEX

Italicized page numbers refer to illustrations.

Roundworms (*cont.*)
  plant destruction, 48,
    53–55, *54*
  reproduction, 49–51

Sand dollars, 96
Scallops, 66, 68, 69
Scavengers, 62, 75, 96
Schistosomes, 45
Scolex, 45–46
Scorpions, 78, 81
Scyphozoa, 33, 35
Sea anemones, 30, 32,
  33, *34*, 35
Sea cucumbers, 96
Sea urchins, 96
Sea wasps, 29, *31*
Segmented worms. *See*
  Annelids
Shrimp, 75
Single-celled organisms,
  13. *See also* Amoebas;
  Protozoans
Slugs, 67, 71
Snails, 66, 67, 71, 72
Species, 11
Spicules, 26–27
Spiders, 78–79, *80*,
  81–82
Spiracles, 84
Sponges, 21–28, *22, 24*
  feeding behavior,
    25–26, 27
  reproduction,
    27–28

supporting structure,
  26–27
Spongin, 26, 27
Squid, 66, 69
Starfish, 95, 97, *98*, 99
Stylet, 52
Surface-to-volume ratio,
  43, 84

Tapeworms, 45–47, *46*
Tentacles, 30, 32, 33, 35,
  37, 69, 71
Termites, 19–20, 87
Ticks, 78, 81
Tracheae, 83–84
Trematodes, 40, 45
Trichinella, 52
Trichinosis, 52
Trypanosomes, 19
Tsetse fly, 19
Tube feet, 96, 97
Tubifex worms, 60
Turbellarians, 40

Vacuole, 15, 17
Vertebrates, 10–11

Webs, spider, 79, *80*, 81
Wings, insect, 89
Wood lice ("pill bugs"),
  76
Worms. *See* Annelids;
  Flatworms;
  Roundworms
Wuchereria bancrofti, 53

ABOUT THE AUTHOR

Nathan Aaseng has written more than 100 books for young people. His subject matter has included science, nature, inventions, sports, and history. He has authored numerous books for Franklin Watts, including *The Common Cold and the Flu*, *Cerebral Palsy*, *Ending World Hunger*, and *Overpopulation: Crisis or Challenge?* He holds a bachelor's degree in English and biology from Luther College, and has worked as a research microbiologist. Mr. Aaseng lives in Eau Claire, Wisconsin, with his wife and four children.

JERICHO PUBLIC LIBRARY

B&T

--
572
A

Aaseng, Nathan.

Invertebrates.

$19.00

5·25·94

DATE			

DISCARD

JERICHO PUBLIC LIBRARY
1 MERRY LANE
JERICHO NY 11753

03/23/1994

BAKER & TAYLOR BOOKS